RUTHIE

A Family's Struggle with ALS

*A story of Amyotrophic Lateral Sclerosis
(ALS, or "Lou Gehrig's Disease")*

LYNN M.

RUTHIE

A Family's Struggle with ALS

LYNN MICLEA

ISBN-10: 1500955833
ISBN-13: 978-1500955830
Library of Congress Control Number: 2014915857
CreateSpace Independent Publishing Platform
North Charleston, South Carolina

Cover photo from Morguefile.com

Acknowledgments

A special thank you goes to my outstanding editor, Vicki Baker, for her amazing word wizardry and wonderful editing magic. All her hours of research, insight, and exceptional judgment are very much appreciated, and her expertise helped to make my words and this story infinitely better. Thank you, Vicki — your help and kindness have been invaluable.

And a deep heart-felt thank you goes to my amazing husband for his extraordinary love, support, and patience, especially during the time that I totally ignored him while writing and rewriting this book. His presence in my world has made my whole life unimaginably better in countless ways, and I will be forever grateful.

DEDICATION

Dedicated with love to my mother, Ruth, who taught me to always love and be kind to people no matter what. Ruth devoted her life to helping others, and I hope that through this book, her life, including her struggle with ALS, will continue to help others, even after her death.

TABLE OF CONTENTS

PREFACE

During the years my mother was ill, starting with her diagnosis and continuing until shortly after her death, I had been sending e-mails to my family back East, updating them as to her condition, and going into detail on her progress. These e-mails were long and comprehensive, and they covered detailed medical information, including her symptoms, struggles, various diagnoses, injuries, ups and downs, difficulties, and deterioration.

They also covered our fears and frustrations, our struggle to find meaning and peace, and our attempts to hold onto a positive attitude. The e-mails contained my own thoughts, perspective, optimism and hope, and they were an attempt to help my family keep my mother in their hearts with love and healing, rather than with pity and despair. As a testament to her battle and struggle with ALS, I kept every e-mail that I had sent.

After she died, I felt compelled to tell her story in book form. After a few attempts and not quite knowing how to go about it, I finally took an online writing class, where I found the motivation and determination to move forward and get it all down on paper.

This book is the result, and it was written straight from my heart. All the parts of this story are true, although a few minor details have been altered to help the reading and flow of the narrative and to fill in details where they were missing.

Please also note that in order to protect the privacy of those involved, all names have been changed except for mine and my mother's. Hospital names, other than the Mayo Clinic, have also been changed.

INTRODUCTION

My beautiful and loving mom, Ruth, passed away in April 2009. She had ALS; she was 81 years old.

Ruth had grown up in the 1920s and 1930s in a loving, family-oriented home in New York. Although she always wanted to please others and make peace, being the oldest of three sisters helped mold her into a strong and independent woman. She was intelligent and driven, and she wanted to make a difference in the world. She became an occupational therapist and devoted her working career to helping others. However, when it came to men, she was somewhat shy and not very confident, and she took more of a back seat, looking for a man to help make the important decisions. Eric fit that bill, and he swept her off her feet. He was attracted to her warmth, humor, and the way she played the piano. She liked his head of wavy blond hair, and she found him to be dynamic and charming, and very comfortable taking control of situations in which she felt insecure. He seemed to be exactly what she was looking for. They fell in love and were married in 1947, when Ruth was just 19.

Most of their marriage was happy, although as Ruth grew more confident in her own judgment and abilities, there were occasional conflicts with Eric, who still liked to be in control and in charge. However, Ruth always wanted everyone happy, and she often backed down to keep the peace.

Ruth and Eric had two children, Stu and Lynn (me). Stu was brilliant, making a successful career in astrophysics. He tended to avoid conflicts and generally looked the other way when tensions arose. I was a sensitive child, disturbed by the presence of anger and conflict. I wanted everything fair and kept trying to stand up for what I believed in, only to butt heads with my father, who kept trying to exert his control. In most of my parents' conflicts, I tended to side with my mother, and I always admired her practicality, strength, and independence. Although the dynamics were sometimes volatile, overall there was a lot of love and support in our family.

ALS had a big impact on all of us. Amyotrophic lateral sclerosis, also known as ALS, or Lou Gehrig's disease, is a progressive and fatal motor neuron disease. In ALS, motor neuron cells in the spinal cord and bulb, or lower brainstem, degenerate and die, impacting the related voluntary muscles. Those muscles, without appropriate nerve impulses, get progressively weaker, until they atrophy and become useless. In 75 percent of those with ALS, the limbs are affected first and initial symptoms include weakness in the arms or legs. In about 25 percent of cases, the bulbar muscles — those used for talking, chewing, and swallowing — are affected first.

Whichever areas are impaired at the onset, weakness eventually spreads to other voluntary muscles. As the disease progresses, the patients generally get weaker and may lose strength in their arms or legs. They may become unable to walk or use their arms or hands. They may lose the ability to speak, chew, or swallow. They may have muscle tremors. Their lungs may get weaker, making it more difficult to breathe. Many choose to use a feeding tube to help get adequate nutrition and keep up their strength. Many choose to go on a ventilator to help them breathe better and prolong their life. And many also reject these devices.

Diagnosis is difficult, as many other diseases have similar symptoms and there is no single test to confirm ALS. My mother, as with most ALS patients, went to many doctors and endured many different tests, trying to find out what was wrong. It often becomes a long process of ruling out other diseases until ALS is all that is left.

The average age of onset is fifty to seventy years old. However, it has been known to attack people in their twenties as well as those in their eighties.

Primary lateral sclerosis (PLS) is another motor neuron disease in the ALS family. PLS is more rare than ALS, and it is caused primarily by upper motor neuron degeneration, whereas ALS is caused by both upper and lower motor neuron degeneration. Upper motor neuron degeneration causes spasms and weakness in the voluntary muscles, which can be uncomfortable or difficult, but in most cases, PLS is not fatal. Lower motor neuron degeneration, as with ALS, causes muscle wasting and atrophy, which eventually affects the respiratory system, and it is fatal. Symptoms of PLS may include difficulty with balance, weakness and stiffness in the legs, and clumsiness. Other symptoms may include involuntary muscle spasms in the hands, feet, or legs; foot dragging; and difficulties with speaking, chewing, and swallowing. PLS progresses gradually over a number of years or even decades. It can sometimes be difficult to differentiate a slowly progressing form of ALS from PLS.

ALS is progressive and fatal. There is no known cause (although it is known to be inherited in some cases), no treatment (other than possibly slowing the disease progression in some cases), and no cure. For most ALS patients, death usually occurs three to five years from the time of diagnosis. For some, it is even less time; however, some people live longer than ten years.

Symptoms, severity, and speed of progression can vary fairly widely among patients.

These diseases are horrible and devastating, and my heart goes out to anyone and any family that is touched by them.

1

THE FIRST DIAGNOSIS

Feeling a choking sense of anxiety rising up from my gut, I looked at my mom. I did not want to see her like this, but I could not look away. With trembling hands, I reached toward her to gently hold her and tell her I loved her, but she sharply pulled back, and pointed toward the other side of the room and shrieked again. What was wrong? What did she want? She shrieked again, pointing with agitation and intensity. I had no idea what she wanted, and I felt a knot in my throat. Feeling helpless, I looked away.

Although we had begun to notice something was wrong about eight years earlier, it was brought into sharp focus just ten months ago. I had suspected something was wrong, but I had been ignoring the signs, hoping they were just a figment of my imagination and would go away. I did not want to consider the possibility that there might be something seriously wrong. My mom's speech had been slowing down. It had been coming out labored, one slow syllable at a time. She was in her seventies, and I kept telling myself that she was simply getting older, that old people talk slower, and it's okay. I knew in my heart that wasn't true, and I had been hearing her speech get slower, more labored, and progressively worse over the past few years. But I didn't want to face it. Even when other people asked if I had noticed that my mom's speech was slow, I carelessly brushed it off with a dismissive response. But alone, in private, I was worried.

My mom had recently been to many doctors, speech therapists, neurologists, and various other specialists, and she had had many tests performed on her, but no one knew what was wrong. Finally, in desperation, on a cloudy day in late October, she went to the Mayo Clinic in Phoenix, Arizona, hoping to get some answers.

My father drove her to the clinic, about six hours away from their home in Camarillo, California. They spent an entire day there, seeing various doctors who subjected my mom to various tests.

The following day, my dad called me at my home in Los Angeles. "We just got back from the Mayo Clinic," he told me. I heard paper crinkling and knew he was reading something he had written down. "They said she has 'progressive bulbar palsy.'" He read the words slowly, and I could tell he did not know what they meant. He waited for a response.

"I don't know what that is," I replied, not knowing what else to say, as I scribbled the words down on a piece of paper.

"Neither do I," he responded. His voice was quiet, silently asking questions that I could not answer.

After hanging up, I went online and did some research on progressive bulbar palsy. What I found made my stomach churn with nausea. Words and phrases bombarded me — progressive, ALS, fatal, weakness, paralysis, feeding tubes, ventilators, death. I tried multiple sites, hoping that at least one of them would say something positive that I could hang onto. But all of them said the same thing. Those words clanged in my head in deep, depressing, ominous tones. I sat there for a while, taking shallow breaths, in shock and disbelief, not sure what to think.

I wondered how much of what I found I should share with my parents. But my stomach was in knots and my throat felt constricted. How could I tell them that most patients with ALS die within three to five years from the onset of symptoms, and that it's even worse for those with progressive bulbar palsy – those patients often die within one to three years from the onset of symptoms? Although we were now first seriously looking into her condition, she really had had symptoms for about eight years already, when we had first noticed her speech getting slower. I did not want to make things more difficult, so I decided to keep this to myself. And maybe the Mayo Clinic was wrong, maybe she had something different. Maybe they had made a mistake.

I tried not to think about the diagnosis, but the words I had read kept popping up in my mind throughout the week. I discussed it briefly with Dustin, my husband, but I found it hard to talk about.

On a cool and cloudy day in early November, the phone rang, interrupting my thoughts. It was my mom. "Come. On. Sa-tur-day," she stated in her slow, halting speech. "I. Have. A. Let-ter. From. The. Ma-yo. Clin-ic."

My stomach tightened. The letter from the Mayo Clinic would have a more definitive diagnosis. Anxiety gripped me, and I wiped my sweaty palms on my jeans. I wasn't sure I wanted to know.

"Okay, we'll be there," I replied quietly, hoping my voice didn't betray my fears.

Saturday arrived cool and crisp. I looked at Dustin nervously, and we got into the car quietly. Dustin looked at me, squeezed my arm with his hand, and nodded. After ten years of marriage, he knew how to calm me down. But even with his support, my stomach was gripped with tension during the 40-minute drive to my parents' house. My mind kept racing over fears and possibilities. We arrived at the retirement community where they lived in Camarillo, showed my entry pass to the man in the guard booth, and the wooden bar was slowly raised.

Entering the retirement community was like entering a different world, with everything in slow motion. The maximum speed limit in the complex was 25 miles per hour, and it was frustrating to drive so slowly, especially after driving at freeway speeds. Creeping forward at a snail's pace, my hands restlessly tapped on the steering wheel as I drove down the main road, passing many modern one-story homes, each looking pretty much like the one before it.

Finally arriving at my parents' house, I parked the car in front and sat there for a minute, feeling icy tentacles of fear in my belly. I glanced at Dustin, and he reached over and gently squeezed my arm. Then hesitantly, I got out of the car. Dark gray clouds obscured the sun, and a brisk cold air came out of nowhere, stinging my face. Dry brown leaves swirled around in the air as I locked the car door.

We slowly walked up the path to the front door, past the familiar bright blue hydrangea flowers, and rang the bell. I listened to the doorbell chiming inside, as my stomach churned.

The door sprang open and both my parents, Eric and Ruth, were standing there, smiling as though nothing was wrong.

"Lynn, come in, come in, it's good to see you," my father happily chanted.

I looked at my mother. She smiled, but the smile did not reach her eyes.

"Come. In," she slowly stated. "I. Have. A. Let-ter." Her speech was even slower than I remembered, and I listened to her tongue tripping over each syllable. I could tell it took a lot of effort for her to speak, as she tried to get out each sound, and it made my heart ache.

We walked into their den and waited for her to come back with the letter. This room always looked old to me — worn beige carpeting and tired-looking furniture.

My mother was a voracious reader and today, as always, there was a pile of paperback books on an end table at the far end of the couch, her favorite place to sit and read. As I started looking at the titles of the books she was reading, she entered the den and handed me a letter printed on white paper. My hand trembled as I took it.

Slowly my eyes focused on the printed words, as the paper shook in my hands. The letter stated that there were two suspected diagnoses: progressive bulbar palsy and bulbar ALS.

I glanced at my mother and I suddenly realized that she was thinner than I had ever seen her.

"Mom," I asked her, "have you lost weight?"

She nodded, and slowly said, "For-ty. Pounds."

I gasped and swallowed hard. "Are you eating okay?"

"Soft. Foods," she responded, and she waved at me to follow her into the large, bright kitchen. "Look," she said, showing me cans of Ensure in chocolate, her favorite flavor. She opened the refrigerator and pointed, and I saw egg salad, pudding, and cottage cheese. Soft foods. She nodded at me like this was good and explained everything.

She grabbed a pen and searched for a pad of paper. Holding the pen at an awkward angle, she wrote, "It's hard to chew."

Then she grabbed the paper back and added, "I can't drink water; it makes me choke."

I felt my eyes open wider and I read the words again. It suddenly hit me that her handwriting had also changed. It was choppy, the lines shaky, not at all like the smooth, flowing script that she used to have. Alarm bells went off in my mind, but I didn't want to think about that now.

I glanced at my father, noticing the few stray wisps of gray hair sticking out from the top of his head. He was watching me, searching for answers, hoping I could help him make sense of everything.

"Mom, sit down and talk to me. Tell me how you're feeling."

She looked at me and slowly nodded, and we sat down in the den. She wrote down how it was getting harder to talk and how frustrating it was. She would keep trying, but it was so hard to get out words and sentences. She said it was also getting harder to eat, but she could manage with that. She wrote that she didn't know what to do. I saw the sadness in her face, which now looked more pale than normal.

"Mom, I'm so sorry. This is awful. Please know that we love you and we're here for you. You are not in this by yourself." I reached for her hand and squeezed it. She looked at me somberly and nodded.

I glimpsed Dustin's face, a mixture of sadness and compassion.

"We'll get you a computer," I told her, brightening up. Her face looked questioningly at me. I glanced at Dustin, and he nodded. "I know you like to talk on the phone to your two sisters back in New York and to friends, but since that is getting too difficult for you, you can e-mail them instead. Can you type?"

She grinned and held up her two index fingers. "With two fingers?" I smiled back at her. "Well that's okay, it will be slow, but you will at least be able to communicate and stay in touch with everyone. This will help." She nodded. I smiled at her and squeezed her arm.

Throughout the afternoon, I noticed my mother try to talk, get frustrated, and then write a few words in her choppy, spiky handwriting. Memories of past visits filled my head, and I recalled my mother animated and happily talking about anything and everything. I knew that she was smart and quick-witted and had a strong opinion on every topic of conversation, and she had always passionately expressed her thoughts. And now here she was barely able to get out a few words at a time.

At the end of the day, as we hugged each other good-bye, I promised them that Dustin and I would be back the next weekend for my mother's birthday.

All week long I worried about my mother. I did more research on the Internet, but found it depressing and quickly gave up. *One step at a time*, I told myself. *Let's just deal with where we are now.*

The next weekend, Dustin and I drove back to my parents' house. "Happy birthday, Mom!" I told her happily, when she answered the door. She was now 79 years old. She seemed happy, and I saw that she had on her usual brown sandals and white socks. She was smiling, but I noticed that her smile was now somewhat weak and crooked, as though she was losing control of the muscles in her face.

After sitting in the den and exchanging pleasantries for a few minutes, I held up some brightly wrapped boxes.

"Open your gifts," I said happily. Her eyes lit up and she took the boxes. She tore open the wrapping of the first gift and grunted at the scented hand cream. With the distorted smile on her face, she opened the cap and rubbed some cream on her arm and smelled it. Her smile grew bigger and she nodded. Then she tore off the wrapping on the second gift and saw pads of paper in pretty colors and a whole box of ballpoint pens. "We don't want you having to search for pens and paper — so you can keep these everywhere and always have them easily in reach, okay?" She nodded and put them aside on the couch.

The four of us chatted away the afternoon. At times my mother spoke haltingly, and at times she wrote notes on pieces of paper.

"Mom, we love you," I told her. "No matter what happens, we're here for you, and we love you." She looked at me and nodded in response. "I know this is awful for you, I know you like to talk." She nodded vigorously. "I'm so sorry, I know it's frustrating. Just please know that we love you."

We went out to a coffee shop for dinner, and my mother ordered spaghetti, which was soft enough for her to eat without much chewing. The waiters then brought out chocolate cake and ice cream and sang *Happy Birthday* to her. She struggled to blow out the candle, but she had no problem eating the cake and ice cream, looking like a happy little kid. We noticed some of the ice cream dripping down her face as she ate. We pointed that out to her and she quickly wiped it off her chin.

As we got ready to leave, we let my parents know that we would be back two weeks later on Thursday for Thanksgiving. I held on to her longer than usual when we hugged good-bye.

Jumbled thoughts and feelings tossed through me as we drove home. What could we do to help her? I had no idea.

2

SHARING THE NEWS

Thanksgiving Day arrived, bright and sunny, and Dustin and I drove back to my parents' house. I knew that my mother's youngest sister, Fran, had come out from New York to visit and stay for a week, and I eagerly looked forward to seeing her. In addition to being sisters, my mom and Fran were best friends. She had a great sense of humor, and I knew that if anyone could help my mom laugh and feel good, it would be Fran.

We walked quickly to their front door, my eyes squinting in the bright sunlight. A brisk, cool wind made my hair fly in all directions, and I kept trying to grab at my hair and put it back in place.

My dad greeted us at the door, welcomed us in, and took our coats. I could hear Fran in the kitchen busily banging pots and pans around, and we went into the kitchen, excited to see her.

Fran's bright red hair was pulled back in a ponytail, and she was wearing an apron. Her face broke into a big smile when she saw us. "Lynn, Dustin, hi, how are you?" She happily greeted us, and gave each of us a big, warm hug.

Fran was the best cook I knew. "Look," she proudly said in her New York accent, "I've been putting food in the blender and the food processor for Ruthie, so she'll have plenty of soft food that she can eat. And I made soup — look. She'll have enough to eat for a month. I'm gonna freeze some of it, too, so she'll have food for a while." She showed me bags and bowls and pots filling the refrigerator and freezer.

"You're the best, Fran. This is a huge help for her!" I felt myself choke up. "Did you make Thanksgiving dinner, too?" I asked hopefully. I loved her cooking.

"Of course," Fran said quickly, "what did you think, I would forget about that? I made stuffing, mashed potatoes, yams with marshmallows — all soft foods. Ruthie can eat it. And a turkey is in the oven; it should be done in about a half hour. We'll eat then. Lynn, Dustin, and Eric, you can help me set the table." I smelled the rich, warm aromas of her cooking filling the air, and I suddenly realized I was starving.

Putting out the plates and silverware, I watched Fran stirring something on the stove, and I noticed my mother looking happy and content. I had not seen her this relaxed and at peace in a long time. *This is so good for her,* I thought.

"Mom," I said, walking into the den, where my mother sat next to her stack of paperback books, "what are you reading now?"

With a big smile, she held up a Dean Koontz book. I could tell that she was enjoying it. We both loved reading action thrillers, and we often traded books back and forth.

"Are you finished with any books I can have?" She nodded and handed me two books — one by Robin Cook and one by James Patterson. "Great," I said happily, looking forward to diving into the books right away. I put the books next to my purse so I wouldn't forget them when it was time to leave.

Looking at my mother and seeing how thin she was, I asked, "Mom, have you shown Fran the letter from the Mayo Clinic?" She shook her head no. "Does she know? Mom, you're going to have to tell her. She needs to know." My mother just looked back at me blankly.

"Dinner's ready," we heard Fran call, and we got up and went into the dining room.

The five of us sat down around the dining room table, my husband and I sitting at the far side of the table, my father at the head of the table, and my mother and Fran at the side of the table closest to the kitchen, so Fran could easily run back and forth with the food.

There was a bowl of soup on each plate. "It's my famous cauliflower soup," Fran said to our puzzled faces. We all tried it, slowly at first, and then quickly finished it, enjoying the rich taste and texture. We helped Fran clear the soup bowls, and then we brought out dish after dish of foods for our Thanksgiving feast — mashed potatoes, sweet potatoes, stuffing, vegetables, and cranberry sauce. Other than the turkey, everything was soft food so that my mother could easily eat it. I looked at the multitude of dishes and couldn't wait to dig in.

Fran put a bib on my mother, and the gesture touched me. Although she was very slow, my mom was able to eat the entire meal, and that warmed my heart. Stuffing our faces and chattering away, we enjoyed the feast, forgetting for a while that there was anything wrong.

After dinner, while Fran, Dustin, and my father cleaned up and did the dishes, I talked to my mother. She still had not told Fran or anyone other than my husband and me what the diagnosis was. Fran was here helping her, but she didn't know the entire story or what was really wrong. She didn't know how serious it was. My mother was keeping herself isolated and I knew that wasn't good.

"Tell her," I pleaded with my mother. "She has a right to know. She's your sister and your best friend. Your family cares about you and loves you. Don't stay hidden and alone with this." My mother had tears in her eyes, and she looked down at her fingers. "Mom," I continued, "let her in. Don't wait until she goes back to New York. Tell her before she leaves so you can cry together and hold each other. She needs to know."

My mom looked up at me and slowly nodded, and she reached for a pen and paper. She wrote, "I can't do it. You tell her."

Walking into the kitchen, I saw that Fran was finishing up and wiping down the counters. "Fran," I said softly, and she looked up at me. Her face fell as she saw the bleak look in my eyes. "We received a letter from the Mayo Clinic. We know what the diagnosis is."

Fran looked at me expectantly, and I heard my mother crying in the den.

"The letter says that she has either progressive bulbar palsy or bulbar ALS," I began. "It's in the ALS family. It's a motor neuron disease. Her muscles will get weaker and waste away. She could end up needing a feeding tube or a ventilator to help her breathe." As I explained the diagnosis and what it meant, I heard my mother's sobs grow louder in the other room. I found it hard to continue talking, but I had to tell Fran the truth. "It's progressive," I told her. I waited a few beats, then softly added, "It's fatal."

Fran's face grew pale and she looked at me blankly, hearing my mother's wails of anguish coming from the den. "You mean she could die from this?"

"Yes," I answered softly, hearing the inconsolable sounds of my mother sobbing loudly, her wails reaching a crescendo of misery.

"Ruthie," Fran whispered, and I watched her move toward my mother, her arms open, embracing her, her sobs matching my mother's. I saw them clutching tightly to each other, crying together, as a choke rose up into my throat.

3

DETERIORATION AND DENIAL

A few weeks later, in early December, Dustin and I went back to visit my mom. Fran was gone, but I was glad to see that my mother's freezer still had many bags of food that her sister had cooked for her.

"Look Mom," I said happily, as Dustin wheeled in a large box. "We brought you a computer!" My mother watched as my husband set up the computer on a small table in the den next to their desk, hooked it up, and got it running. Then we sat with her and showed her how to turn the computer on and off, how to get online, and how to send e-mails. She was slow, and it was difficult and tedious for her, but she took notes and seemed to understand. We made her go through the entire process a few times on her own and send a few e-mails so that we knew she could do it and she would feel comfortable. At least now she had a way of staying in touch with everyone without having to talk.

"Do you like the computer? Will you use it?" I looked at her expectantly.

"Arghzjaaaaahhh," she said.

"What? I don't understand you," I responded, looking at her, shocked and confused.

"Ahaajrgheeeeee," she said more intently.

Anxiety flooded through my body, and I realized her speech was now coming out garbled. "Write it down," I pleaded, looking for a pen and paper.

Her speech had deteriorated further. It was no longer just slow; it was now unintelligible. Her tongue was not working well anymore.

She thrust the paper at me, and I saw a few words scrawled on it. "I type slow," she had written.

"That's okay," I told her, "you can still communicate, even if it's slow. And you will receive e-mails back from people, and that will be good to read. So even if you're slow, you can still stay in touch with everyone. This will be great for you."

She nodded.

Throughout that day, I watched as my mom kept trying to speak, and I saw her getting increasingly frustrated and angry. It had always been so natural for her to just easily say whatever she wanted at any time. Now she kept trying, thinking she still could speak if she wanted. But it kept coming out garbled and her distress increased.

"Mom, write it down," I told her over and over. But she wanted to speak so badly, and she kept trying. I handed her paper and a pen, but she continued to try to talk. Each time she tried, only unintelligible noises came out. She finally shrieked and threw the paper and pen across the room. Collapsing on the couch in the den, she dissolved into frustrated tears.

A few minutes later, after she had calmed down, I pulled my chair closer to her. "Mom, have you noticed anything else with your body? Any weakness or confusion?"

She thought for a moment, and then shook her head no. I was relieved at that. Maybe it wouldn't get any worse. *If it stays like this and doesn't progress, we can live with it,* I thought.

That evening, we went out to dinner. The air was chilly and we took our coats. Walking from the parking lot to the coffee shop, I noticed that my parents were walking slower than usual. But they seemed stable, so I didn't think too much of it.

We all slid into a booth. My mother ordered soft food by pointing to the menu. We tried to keep the conversation upbeat and not dwell on her illness. While we ate, I noticed that some of the food kept dropping back out of her mouth onto the plate. And then I noticed some drool falling and dripping into the food on her plate. She didn't seem to notice, and she kept eating. *Leave her alone and let her be,* I thought. She ate less than usual, about half her food, and then she got a box to take the rest home.

After we got back to their house, I saw a tear roll down my mother's cheek. "What is it?" I asked her.

She took one of the new pens and wrote on a yellow sheet of paper, "Look what's become of me." I handed her a tissue, as I saw her tears falling onto her blouse.

I took her hand and looked in her eyes. "Mom," I told her earnestly, "I want to remind you that you are *not* your body, and you are *not* your disease." I paused to make sure she was hearing me. "You are still the special, loving, intelligent, and interesting person that you've always been." My mother looked at me intently as I was speaking. "You're the amazing and wonderful *you* inside your body. And that will never change. Your body may give out in various ways. But that is not *you*. And Mom, you are very special." I looked at her, and she nodded. "You are still the same person inside and we will always love you. Please don't forget that."

She looked back at me, clearly focused and listening to every word, as she dabbed at her eyes, crying softly. I hoped she really understood and would remember what I was saying.

"Look," I said, "I brought you something else that might help you." She looked up at me, and I handed her two sheets of paper. One was a list of emotions: happy, blah, tired, scared, depressed, angry, and a few others. "This is so that you can just point to an emotion you're feeling rather than trying to say it or write it down each time. That should make it easier to let people know how you're feeling. Would that help?" She nodded, pointed to "happy," and laughed.

"And this one," I explained, pointing to the second piece of paper, "is a list of tasks that you might need help with. You can point to one of them, and Dad will know what to help you with." She looked at the list, which included cooking, dishes, laundry, food shopping, and a few others. My mom nodded at that one also, and she put both lists on an end table, within easy reach.

My father picked up the sheets of paper and briefly looked at them. "What do you mean," he said, "I have to help her with these? I don't have to do these, that's her job."

I wasn't sure if he was joking or serious. "Dad, she might need help with some of those. You're her husband; you have to help her."

My father dramatically clutched at his chest as though stricken, and said, "Oh no, you mean I really have to help her?" He then had a big, stupid grin on his face, and I realized he was just joking.

He obviously thought he was being funny. Inside, though, I thought there might be some truth underneath his joking and I hoped that he truly would help her. I knew that he really did consider those things "women's work" and he had never done any of those tasks himself. When he joked around like this, it was hard to know what he actually thought and what he would do. I didn't want to create any tension, so I didn't push further.

I needed to change the topic, and I felt somewhat reluctant to bring it up. I looked at my mother and quietly said, "I also found a support group that might help you. It's an ALS support group that meets once a month." She nodded at me, and I continued. "They meet locally, maybe twenty minutes from here, and they offer all kinds of support, referrals, devices, and evaluations. Their next meeting is in two weeks. It looks like it might be beneficial. Do you think that might help you? Would you like to try it?"

My mother's eyes lit up, and she nodded. I was glad that she wanted to go.

I glanced at my father. His face clouded over and he said harshly, "She does not have ALS and she does not need a support group."

"But her diagnosis is in the ALS family, and they might have other information there that could assist her."

"She doesn't need a support group," he sternly repeated.

"She's isolating herself," I insisted. "Here she would see and be with other people in a similar position, dealing with a lot of the same issues. I think it might be beneficial for her."

My father looked over at my mother. "Do you want to go?" he asked her.

She nodded yes, and I felt elated. "Family members can come too," I explained, "so we can all go together, okay?" My mother nodded and smiled.

That week I kept thinking about the upcoming meeting, wondering what it would be like. Would everyone be disabled? In wheelchairs? Was this the right thing to do? I worried that it might be overwhelming and depressing for my mother.

Later that week, the phone rang. It was my father. "We saw a neurologist," he said with no preamble. "Your mother does not have ALS. She has progressive bulbar palsy. That is not ALS."

"Yes it is," I said sharply. "It's the same thing. It's in the ALS family."

"No, she does not have ALS. Her own doctor said so."

I did not want to argue with him and I let it go.

That weekend I drove over there to discuss it further with them. My mother showed me a letter she had received from her neurologist. I saw that he had written that she "did not meet the criteria for ALS," and that she had progressive bulbar palsy. The letter also stated that he had only seen one or two patients with that diagnosis. To me, it did not seem like he even knew that progressive bulbar palsy was in the ALS family, and it looked like he was just summing up and repeating what was written in the letter from the Mayo Clinic. After all my research, I felt like I already knew more than the neurologist did.

"Mom, go see another doctor. Even if it's progressive bulbar palsy, that's in the ALS family."

"No," my father said, a bit too loud. "She does *not* have ALS."

"Yes she does, it's the same family. Mom, it's still a motor neuron disease. Go see a neurologist who specializes in motor neuron diseases so you can get better help from someone familiar with it."

"*No,*" my father's voice boomed. "She *does not have* ALS!"

Tears stinging my eyes, I clenched my fists in frustration. My father was in denial. He was grasping at and holding onto a lifeline of hope. "She *does not have* ALS!" he repeated like a defiant mantra, glaring at me.

What could I do? It seemed like my mother was beginning to come to terms with having bulbar-onset ALS and was ready to go to a support group. And now, her inexperienced doctor was doing her a disservice by telling her it was *not* ALS. My father was grabbing on to that like a life raft, eagerly moving away from the seriousness of what she did have. To me, that felt like a step backward.

I thought about what I should do. I knew I couldn't force them to see it my way or admit to something they didn't want to look at. Maybe this was too much for them to deal with at this time, and they needed a period of rest from the overwhelming terror of the disease so far. Maybe I needed to pull back and let them process it and think about it.

I decided that I wouldn't push too much right away. If they wanted to cling to the idea that it was not ALS, then let them have hope a little while longer. However, I thought that at some point in the not-too-distant future, they would need to come to terms with it, and it would be a shock all over again. But I knew that they had to deal with it in their own time, when they were ready. So I backed off.

Once home, thoughts swam in circles in my head. *What should I do? Was I doing the right thing? Should I insist that it was really ALS?* I had no idea.

The next week was the ALS support group meeting and I didn't know if my parents were still considering going or not. I e-mailed my mother a few times telling her that I felt it would help her, but she did not respond, and I had no idea what she was thinking or feeling. I did not want to push more than that, since I did not want to press the issue and inadvertently push them away from it.

On the day of the meeting, my father called me. *Uh-oh*, I thought, once I heard his voice.

"What is this meeting today about?" he asked.

"It's an ALS support group meeting for people with ALS, or for family and caregivers of those with ALS," I started to explain.

He interrupted me and shouted angrily into the phone, "She does *not* have ALS!"

"Yes she does!" I shouted back. "What she has is in the ALS family and the meeting could help her."

"Then you tell me," he yelled, with rage in his voice, "which doctor who has examined your mother told you that she has ALS."

"I've done a lot of research..." I began.

"No, I don't care about research. What doctor told you that she has ALS? Who did you speak to?"

"Dad, you're not listening to me."

His voice got even louder, "She does *not* have ALS! You tell me what doctor..."

Shaking and furious, I slammed the phone down, hanging up on him. He was impossible! Why wouldn't he listen to me? Why was he so blind and stupid? Why would he deny my mother the support she needed and wanted? She was willing to go, and she was the one with the disease. How could he stand in her way of going? I sank into a chair, put my face in my hands, and felt my eyes burning with tears.

4

THE FIRST
SUPPORT GROUP MEETING

One hour before the meeting was to start, I called my father back, feeling a bit scared. How angry at me was he? Would he even talk to me now?

As soon as he answered the phone, I started talking right away to get in what I wanted to say before he could stop me. "Hi, it's me. I can come out there, pick up Mom, and I will take her to the meeting. You don't have to go. But please don't stop her if she wants to try it. I'll take her."

Holding my breath, I waited for his response. I desperately wanted her to get the support she needed, no matter which one of us took her, even if I had to drive out of my way.

"I'll take her," my father finally said softly. "We can meet there." He sounded very subdued.

"Good, I'm glad you're going. I'll see you there." I let out a big breath. I said good-bye and quickly got off the phone before he could change his mind.

Feeling relieved, I looked for the directions and got ready to go. Dustin came with me, and on the thirty-minute drive to the meeting place, my mind went over the past few conversations with my father. I knew he had a tendency to be stubborn, to bury his head in the sand and not see things, and to be angry and controlling. It made me wonder what I could expect from him in the near future in terms of support for my mother. I hoped his denial would not last long and that we could count on him to help her and put her needs first, but I had my doubts.

We arrived at the address, and turned into a long, steep, black paved driveway, curving upwards. At the top it leveled off and opened up into a small parking lot, with parking spaces along one side, and a building on the other side. We easily found a parking spot, got out, and turned, looking at the building.

Facing us was a squat, one-story, U-shaped, sterile-looking government building. We looked at it, wondering where the meeting would be. In the center, in the main part of the building, we saw a fairly large room with glass walls, and a woman was in there setting up chairs. I wondered if that was the meeting room. We tried one door, but it was locked. We walked to a second door and that one opened when we tugged on it.

We slowly entered the room and watched the woman unfold another chair and place it next to the others. I hesitated, and then in a soft, timid voice asked the woman, "Is this the ALS support group meeting?"

"Yes, yes, welcome, come in!" she said, her black hair bouncing as she moved her head. "I'm Diane, and I'm just setting up. There are some brochures on the table over there, if you want. We'll be starting in about 15 minutes." She then went back to unfolding the plastic chairs and arranging them in a circle.

We put our jackets across the seats of four of the chairs at the back end of the circle, facing the front of the room. Feeling nervous and uncomfortable, we walked back outside.

The bright sunlight bounced off the car windshields across the parking lot. I tried to take deep, calming breaths. *You can do this,* I told myself. *It will be okay.* After a few minutes, I felt a bit more relaxed, and we went back inside to wait.

My parents had not yet arrived, and I looked over some of the brochures on the table. I hoped my parents had not changed their minds and were still coming.

I had been worried about what we would find. I expected to see people in wheelchairs, on ventilators, in obvious pain, and in varying stages of deterioration. I thought I would see a lot of seriously disabled people. However, as the room started filling up and people took their seats, I was surprised — only one person was in a wheelchair, and I did not notice anyone with an obvious disability. The individuals around us were normal, everyday people, smiling, nodding, or talking among themselves. Were we in the right place?

My parents arrived a few minutes later. We nervously hugged and greeted each other, not saying much, and we then sat down and waited for the meeting to start.

After a short welcoming speech by Diane, who was the leader of the group, we went around the circle, one at a time, introduced ourselves, and gave a little bit of our background. As I listened to each person introduce themselves and share, I realized that these were simply nice, normal people, who happened to be dealing with some muscle weakness and atrophy, just like we were. And it was slightly different for everyone. Some had more weakness in their arms, some had it in their legs, and some had a harder time holding up their head. There was one other person in the circle who could not speak, just like my mom. That man had a special communication device with him, which we later found out was called a Lightwriter, which would speak for him. He typed in whatever he wanted, pushed a button, and the device then audibly repeated the words for him. He was smiling and happy through it all. How wonderful! Seeing others coping with symptoms similar to my mom's gave me an enormous feeling of relief and hope.

Then it was my turn. Nervously, I introduced both myself and my mother, letting everyone know that she could not speak. I briefly outlined her symptoms and progression, and ended with the diagnosis from the Mayo Clinic. My mother nodded along to all of it, while my father sat stone-faced. It felt very supportive and comfortable, and I was really glad that we were there.

Then it was my father's turn. "My name is Eric," he stated. "My wife, Ruth, does not have ALS." Embarrassed, I shrunk down in my chair. *No,* I silently pleaded, *don't say anything else.* But he continued. "Now, I don't care if the rest of you have ALS, but Ruth does not. I want to make that clear. She does not have ALS. Thank you."

I felt my face turn hot with embarrassment. No one else in the group said a word, they just let him speak. Then the next person spoke, and I tried to breathe normally and calm down.

After the introductions, the meeting was opened up to anyone who wanted to share their concerns, questions, stories, and experiences. As the others shared, my mother wrote down a few sentences for me to say for her. I loved that she wanted to contribute to the group and share her concerns, and that she felt comfortable enough to do that. And I also was glad that she gave these to me to read rather than to my father. I read her sentences to the group about excess saliva and drooling and about not liking to eat in front of other people. Everyone in the group, except my father, nodded and understood and offered support and suggestions. It was amazing, almost exhilarating. We found a place where my mother was not a freak. Where she was not only accepted, but where she fit in and where others really understood what she was going through. Many of them shared the same experiences.

By the end of the meeting, I felt like we were all friends. We shared a strong bond. We ended with a group hug, and I didn't want to leave. I couldn't wait for the next meeting.

I gave my name, phone number, and e-mail address to Julie, the case manager for the group, a very sweet and caring lady with a lot of experience dealing with ALS patients and their families. Julie said she would contact me by e-mail the next day so that I could officially register my mother with the group. Once she was registered, we would get mailings, information, and further help from them. It felt like we had come home.

As we walked to our cars in the parking lot after we left the room, I looked at my mother. "Did you like the meeting? Did you find it helpful?"

She nodded enthusiastically, and I was pleased. I did not ask my father what he thought.

The next day, I received the e-mail from Julie, and I immediately filled out the form with all the requested information, and I e-mailed it back to her right away. I also let her know that we wanted a Lightwriter, one of those machines that could talk for her. *Good,* I thought, *we're making progress.*

The following weekend, I went back to my parents' house for a visit. The ALS group had sent my mother a huge packet of information about ALS. My mother had read through it and she showed it to me. There was a lot of information about both ALS and progressive bulbar palsy.

My mother handed me a note saying, "I know progressive bulbar palsy is ALS."

I looked at her and saw sadness in her eyes. I moved to her and hugged her. "Oh, Mom," I murmured. I held her for a long minute before she pulled away.

I sighed with relief. I knew that if she understood what she had, and if she was willing to acknowledge it and face it, that would help a lot in her being able to deal with everything in the months to come.

"Mom, this doesn't mean that you will definitely get limb weakness. You might, but it's not definite. It could stay in the bulbar region and only affect your speech and eating." She looked at me and nodded. Although I wanted her to be realistic, a part of me also wanted her to hang on to whatever hope she could and enjoy her time in the present as much as possible. I did not want her to be overwhelmed by possibilities and what-ifs that might not happen.

"And don't forget," I continued, "your disease is progressing very slowly, slower than normal. It's already been eight years since the onset of your symptoms. So that is good news." She nodded, but I had the feeling that she knew it would progress. Maybe it was already progressing, and she wasn't even telling me how bad it was for her. Maybe I was the one in denial, and she was being more realistic than me. Maybe I was the one trying to hang onto a thread of hope.

5

MORE SYMPTOMS

"Mom, are you still doing volunteer work?" I asked her a couple weeks later during a visit. She nodded yes. I knew that she had been volunteering in a hospital a few days a week.

"What are you doing there? How are you helping them?"

She wrote, "In Radiology, I help file the x-rays."

"That's great! Are you still comfortable doing that? It's not too hard for you?"

She nodded yes, and she smiled. Then she handed me a note, "It's easy and I want to help. I'm enjoying it."

"I'm so impressed you are still doing that. Just know that if it feels like it's too much, it's okay to stop and to stay home. Don't overdo it."

She looked at me and nodded. Then she showed me the latest books she was reading.

"Good, Mom, I love that you are reading and still doing things that bring you pleasure. Don't ever stop that."

She nodded, and then all of us looked at each other. We had planned on playing miniature golf today, and we were itching to get going. "So, are we ready to go?" Everyone got up, excited with anticipation. We all loved playing miniature golf, and we were looking forward to this. It was something we had been doing together as a family for many years.

The four of us piled into my dad's car, and he drove the 25 minutes to the golf course, which was a few miles from the Pacific Ocean. When we arrived and got out of the car, we squinted in the bright sunlight and took deep breaths of the fresh, salty air, which was cooled by the local ocean breezes. We picked up our little golf putters and brightly colored balls, and ambled over to the first hole. We had been coming to this golf course for a long time, and we always had a good time, laughing and cheering each other on.

"Who's first?" my father asked.

"Mom can go first today," I said, and she picked up her orange ball and placed it on the mat. She swung and missed completely, which was not like her. She laughed and tried again, this time hitting the ball. It bounced off a wall just a few feet away and ran out of steam halfway down the path.

We were usually fairly evenly matched, but this time I could see that my mother was having trouble. After the rest of us had already hit our balls into the cup, my mother was still struggling to hit the ball close to the cup. After a few more holes, I realized that my mother's stance was a bit stiff and she was striking the ball awkwardly, with poor control and inconsistent aim. Her coordination seemed to be off. By the sixth hole, I started helping her, kicking her ball closer to the hole after she had hit it. She laughed, but when I looked at her, I noticed her jaw was clenched. At the tenth hole, I watched as she slammed the putter on the ground, her face tight with frustration. By the end of the course, I knew she did not have the same control over her motor skills that she used to have, and it was no longer easy or comfortable for her to play. I could see that she was not having fun or enjoying this like she used to, and I felt sadness swimming in my gut. I knew this would be the last time we ever played miniature golf together.

The phone rang a few days later, and it was my father. "We've been in a car accident."

I was immediately concerned. "When? Are you okay? What happened?"

"Yeah, we're fine, it was last month, and it was your mother's car." *Why hadn't he told me this before?* I asked myself. "It was when we were coming home from the Mayo Clinic in her car," he continued, as though nothing was wrong. "She was driving when we had the accident. Anyway, the car is now fixed and ready, and we need help in picking it up. Could you drive us out there to get the car?"

"Yes, of course," I responded. "When do you want to go?"

"Today," he said. "Now."

I swallowed my anger at his lack of communication. *Why had he not told me about the accident before this? Why had he not given me any notice about driving him there?* Frustrated, I felt my hands knot up into fists. *Let it go,* I thought to myself, releasing my fists and my breath.

"Okay, we'll pick you up in two hours," I replied.

The drive out to pick up their car took close to an hour. I tried talking to my mother. "How are you feeling?" She did not respond. "Are people treating you differently?" There was no response. After a few more questions and not receiving any response from her, I gave up and stopped trying to make conversation with her.

"Dad, how did you get home from here after the accident, if you left your car here?"

"We called a taxi," he said simply.

"You should have called me; I would have come and picked you up."

"It was no big deal, we didn't think it was that far, and it's already done."

My parents filled out paperwork, got their car, and then followed us back to our house. Dustin and I then took them out to a coffee shop for a late lunch.

"Mom, are you feeling okay?"

"She is fine," my father loudly declared. "She does *not* have ALS."

Feeling frustrated and wanting to yell at him that he was not helping at all, I looked helplessly at my mother. She kept eating her soft food, not looking up, drool dripping onto the tablecloth. I did not want to push the issue and make things worse, so I dropped it.

Later, after doing more research both online and in books, I came to realize the different nuances in the varying terminology with ALS, and I realized what the doctor meant when he had written that my mother "did not meet the criteria for ALS." With having problems only in the area of talking or chewing, my mother's condition would be *"most likely"* ALS, but *not* *"definitively"* ALS. If her disease kept progressing and other symptoms appeared, then the diagnosis would be more definitive and concrete and then she *would* "meet the criteria" for ALS. So it just wasn't quite there yet, but the disease was still progressing.

I read that other symptoms could include tremors, trouble swallowing, and significant weakness and atrophy in her arms and/or legs. If my mother developed any of those symptoms, then her diagnosis would move into *"definitively"* ALS. My guess was that it was just a matter of time.

The next time I saw my mother, and each time I saw her after that, I kept asking her if she had any other symptoms.

"Do you have any spasms or tremors?" She shook her head no.

"Have you noticed any leg or arm weakness?" No.

"Have you tripped or fallen recently?" No.

"Have you dropped things or have you had a difficult time lifting things?" No.

"Do you have trouble swallowing?" No.

"Have you choked at all while eating?" No.

"Good," I told her, "these are all good signs that it is not progressing to full-blown ALS at this time. Maybe it never will." My mom just looked at me with no expression.

I guessed that the odds were that it would probably progress, but I still wanted to hold onto hope, for both of us. Maybe it would stay just bulbar, and this would be it. Maybe I wanted to bury my head in the sand and be in denial too, like my father, just for a little while longer.

I received a birthday card in the mail, and at first I did not recognize the handwriting on the envelope. Then I looked at the return address, and with shock, I realized this was my mother's handwriting. It had deteriorated further. Looking at the writing, I could tell that she was having trouble holding the pen. My stomach flipped.

When Dustin and I saw them next, in early January, I gave my mother a few sheets of printed address labels for people in the family.

"Look, Mom," I said, proudly handing her the address labels. "You don't have to try to write addresses anymore. You can just use these labels. It's easy, see? Just let me know when you run out, and I can print more, okay?" She took the labels, but had no other response.

For the next hour, I tried to talk to her more and ask questions, but she was not very communicative. I wasn't sure if she was not up to talking, not feeling well, or if she was not understanding my questions. I finally just let her be.

That evening, we brought out the rummy tile game, which we had always played together for years. She brightened up as we set up the tiles. We each picked our tiles, set up our boards, and started playing. My mother had always done well at this game, but for some reason, she did not seem to understand or see the combinations well this time. She would put down a combination that did not belong together or tiles that did not go together. We gently pointed it out to her, and she took back her tiles and tried again. After a few more errors like that, I started looking at her tiles and helping her. She accepted my help and seemed to enjoy the rest of the game, but it made me wonder if her mental faculties were being affected.

I also knew that she played in a few bridge games with others in the retirement community. I wondered if she was struggling there as well.

I came back to visit again a week later. When the door sprang open, I saw both my parents standing there, smiling. My mother looked alert and happy, and I felt relieved.

After talking to each other in the den for a short while, I brightened up. "Would you like to go to Channel Islands, with the boats and the shops?" I asked hopefully.

My mother nodded happily and went to get her purse. She loved shopping, so this was a treat for her. I loved the boats and the pier and the fresh ocean setting, so this was a treat for me, too. This place had it all, including the best ice cream.

Traffic was light, and we drove for just over a half hour, before pulling into a spot in the large parking area. We got out of the car and squinted into the bright sun. I was glad that I had my sun hat with me, but I had to keep grabbing it in the brisk wind.

"Ahhhh, smell the air," I said, taking a deep breath of the fresh, salty sunshine.

We walked along the path by the edge of the water, admiring all the boats, as they languidly bobbed up and down in the soft waves. Sunlight glinted off the water between the boats, as seagulls squawked overhead. I always loved walking there by the water and the boats, feeling free and open and at peace.

Over the next few hours, we felt like we were simply kids having fun. After looking at the boats, we wandered in and out of many of the gift shops, and my mother bought a small, bright-orange ceramic fish.

We then sat on a bench and sighed, looking out over the water, without needing to say anything, each of us lost in our own thoughts.

"Who wants ice cream?" I asked a short time later. I saw smiles light up their faces, and we got up and walked to the ice cream shop. After a few minutes, we came back out, clutching our ice cream cones like treasured treats. We sat at a small glass table overlooking the bobbing water and contentedly lapped at our cones.

Glancing at my parents' faces, I could see that they were relaxed and happy. It felt like a moment out of time, where we were simply enjoying ourselves, totally forgetting that any illness or difficulty existed. I wished this moment could last forever.

6

Needing a Cane

I met my parents later that month for another ALS support group meeting. This time, I was looking forward to it. Again, I had arrived before my parents and saved seats for them. They arrived a few minutes later, and I watched them slowly making their way in from the parking lot.

I went to greet them, and we hugged. "Hi Mom, how are you feeling?"

She grunted, rolled up her pant leg, and pointed. Looking down at her leg, I gasped audibly. "What happened?" On her knee was a huge bruise, and there was a smaller bruise near her ankle. Worried, I looked up at her face.

"Rraaagjz," she said.

"What? Write it down," I said, fumbling for a pen and paper to give her.

"She fell," my father told me. My mom held up two fingers. "Twice," he added.

"You fell? Twice?" I repeated, sounding stupid to my own ears.

My father waved it away and said, "It was over a couple weeks. She fell twice over the past two weeks. It's no big deal. She's fine."

"What? She's not fine — look at that bruise! That's huge!" I looked at my mom's face, and she tried to give a weak, lopsided smile.

"What happened, Mom? Why did you fall? Were your legs weak?"

She shook her head no and wrote down, "Lost my balance." Then she scribbled some more and handed me the paper. "Need hand rails." Then she added a few more words. "Need bars in the shower."

"You want grab bars put in the shower to hold onto?" She nodded. "Okay, we'll do that, we'll put those in for you." She nodded again.

"I'm worried about you falling again," I told her. "Maybe it would be good to get a cane or a walker or something to help support you so you don't fall again." She looked back at me and hesitated, then she nodded slowly.

Diane then started the meeting, and we took our seats. When it was my turn to share, I told the group about my mother falling a few times. Many people in the group said that she really should get a cane or walker for support right away to help stabilize her so that she wouldn't fall again and hurt herself even more. They said that she could easily break a bone if she falls, and we certainly didn't want that. Several of the people in the group told stories of how they had fallen, and how important it is to prevent falls and to have assistive devices like canes or walkers.

One man emphatically said, "Now is the time to get it, before it gets worse and she really hurts herself." I agreed and my mother nodded. My father said nothing.

On the way home from the meeting, we stopped at my parents' local drugstore so that my mother could pick up her latest prescription.

"Hey," I said to her, "while we're here, let's take a look at the canes and see what they have."

Glancing at my father, I saw his face tighten and cloud with anger, and I quickly looked away.

Where was my mother? There she was — near the greeting cards. She was ignoring my father as well. She smiled at me and nodded, and we both walked over to the section with the canes. I noticed a really nice one for a reasonable price. It had a very comfortable foam-covered handle, it was strong and sturdy, and it had pink roses all over it.

"Look, Mom. What do you think of this one?"

I showed her the pink flowered cane, and she smiled, liking it right away.

"*She doesn't need a cane,*" my father said a little too loudly, walking aggressively toward us.

I ignored him and faced my mother. "Try it," I told her. "Walk around with it and see if it's comfortable." She took the cane and walked around with it a little bit, smiling.

"Do you like it? Is it comfortable? Do you want to get it?" She nodded yes to all my questions.

My father suddenly and powerfully forced his way between us. "*Don't get her a cane,*" he shouted. "*She doesn't need one.*"

"Dad," I calmly explained, "it's just to be safe. We want to support her. We don't want her to fall and hurt herself."

"Ruth doesn't need a cane!" His voice thundered in my ears.

"Even if she doesn't need it now, it's good to have for the future, so she'll be safe," I tried to sound reasonable.

"HOW DARE YOU! PUT THAT AWAY! I SAID SHE DOES NOT NEED A CANE!" His voice boomed throughout the entire store, and I could feel the silence settle like a dense fog in the rest of the store, as people started watching.

I tried to address my mother, but my father kept physically forcing himself between us, blocking me from seeing her. I took a step to one side, but he matched me so that I could not see around him. I tried moving to the other side, but he kept mirroring my steps, and I could not see my mother.

"Mom..." I started to say.

"NO!" he screamed threateningly, *"SHE DOES NOT NEED A CANE!"*

I suddenly self-consciously realized that the entire store was now watching and listening to him as he continued to shout and scream.

I tried one more time to step to the side to see my mother, but he again matched my step and blocked my line of sight.

His face turned red. *"GET AWAY, GET AWAY FROM HER. I SAID NO, SHE DOESN'T WANT A CANE, SHE DOESN'T NEED A CANE!"*

"Mom..."

"NO! YOU'RE TRYING TO MAKE HER SICK! THIS IS YOUR FAULT! YOU'RE THE ONE WHO IS CAUSING THIS! YOU MADE HER

SICK! SHE DIDN'T NEED A CANE BEFORE YOU STARTED THIS! YOU DID THIS TO HER!"

Trembling with a combination of fear, embarrassment, and anger, I looked at my father. "You're so confused and miserable..." I started to say.

"YOU'RE HORRIBLE! YOU'RE SCUM!" he screamed even louder, interrupting me. And suddenly, he lunged at me. I saw his fists clenched and his body powerfully storming toward me.

My muscles tightened, my stomach knotted up, and then the memories of fear and horror from my childhood rapidly bombarded me — images of the intense madness all over his face, the sound of his hand powerfully striking my skin... the hitting, the pain, and the pitifully shrieking sounds of my own screams... of his voice yelling, "I'll give you a beating you'll never forget!"... memories of hot, searing agony... I could still feel the agonizing blows on my skin, the sharp, stinging pain... I could still hear my own wails and sobs... A whirlwind of images and sounds enveloped me, transporting me in time to a terrifying world of horror, and I felt dizzy. A choking sensation rose into my throat, and I quickly coughed, hoping to keep down the nausea that was now building.

And now here I was, in my fifties, in a public drugstore, and he was coming at me again. Noooooo! Instinctively, my arms came up to protect myself. Attempting to stop him, I chokingly said, "Don't you dare touch me, or I'll fight back." Of course, I knew that whatever he did, I would never hit him, but I felt the need to try to stand up for myself. Maybe that would scare him and shock him out of it and he would stop.

However, this infuriated and enraged him further. His arms came up, and he shook his fists over his head and lunged at me. Three inches from my face, he screamed with a diabolical intensity, *"COME ON, THAT'S WHAT I WANT, YEAH, LET'S DO IT, COME ON!"*

Visibly shaking, feeling overwhelmingly horrified and terrorized, I turned and walked away, my mouth dry, vomit rising into my throat.

Without another word, I left the store and drove home, shaking uncontrollably.

7

Trying to Help

After that episode in the drugstore, I tried to reach my mother by e-mail instead of by telephone so that I would not have to talk to my father. I sent her a message and told her that we loved her and wanted to help and support her. "You don't have to live like that," I typed to her. "We love you and you can come live with us at any time. Think about it. And please go back and get the pink cane; you need it for balance and safety." She did not respond.

The phone rang the following day, and it was my father. "I'm sorry I yelled at you in the store," he said, and I felt too raw to respond. He continued, "I have decided that I will allow her to get the cane."

Allow, I thought? She needs *permission* to get a cane? I held my tongue and did not respond to that part. "Good, I'm glad. She needs it," I finally said quietly.

We went back to visit my parents the next weekend, and my mom happily showed me the pink flowered cane, which she had gotten that week. She nodded proudly, with a weak, crooked smile, and she then put the cane in a corner.

"Mom, make sure you use it," I said. She nodded absently.

We then went to Home Depot and picked out some grab bars for her shower. Dustin spent the afternoon installing them, while I tried to talk to my mother.

"Mom, how are you feeling?" She did not respond.

"Where are your lists of emotions? Remember those?" She stared blankly at me.

"Are you using the lists or the address labels?" No response.

Just as I was ready to give up trying to talk to her, my mother grabbed paper and a pen. After scribbling a few words, she handed me the paper. "Dad won't help me."

"He won't help you with what? What do you need?" I asked.

She wrote some more words. "Everything. He ignores me."

I felt like my heart was breaking. "Does he help with the dishes?" She shook her head no. "With the laundry?" No. "With food shopping?" She wrote more words. "He drives me there and waits outside." I felt anger rising in my gut.

"Dad," I said, and he came into the room.

"What?" He looked at me as though I was bothering him.

"Are you helping Mom with anything?"

"I help her all the time," he said dismissively, like what I was saying was nonsense.

"Do you help with the dishes?"

"She doesn't need help with the dishes, she can do the dishes."

I glanced at my mother, and she was shaking her head no.

"Do you help with the laundry?"

"No, I will not do laundry. That's your mother's job."

I saw tears welling up in my mother's eyes.

"Maybe these tasks are getting to be too much for her, Dad. Maybe she needs your help."

He looked at my mother. "Do you need help?" She raised her face to him and nodded, as a tear ran down her cheek.

"Okay, I'll help her. But not the laundry. That's her job."

"So you'll help her with the dishes and with food shopping?"

He hesitated, then said, "Okay, I'll help her with those."

It felt like we were begging and twisting it out of him, but I figured it's a start. Maybe he would help a little more from now on, but I wasn't sure he really would.

Julie, the ALS case manager, came out in early February to meet with my parents and me. We immediately remembered her from the support group meetings. She was warm and friendly and discussed her own background and what the local ALS chapter could do for my mother. She then asked my mother questions so that she could assess my mother's needs.

"Are you comfortable living here?" she asked, addressing my mother.

"Yes, she's fine, there's no problem," my father answered right away.

Julie glanced at him and then looked back at my mother. "Is there anything you need that would help you?"

"No, she doesn't need anything," my father sternly responded. "Everything is fine. She doesn't need any help." He folded his arms over his chest and glared at Julie.

"Eric, I'd like to hear from Ruth," Julie said softly. "Ruth, do you need hand rails or grab bars or anything to..."

My father interrupted her, his voice getting louder. "I told you she doesn't need anything!"

"My husband put in grab bars for her, so she now has them," I said, and Julie smiled at me.

"Are you eating okay? Are you losing weight?" Julie asked my mother kindly.

"She's fine," my father answered. "In fact, all the other women here are asking how they can get this disease so they can lose weight, too." He then chuckled at his joke, looking at each of our faces to see if we were laughing and impressed with his humor. Horrified and embarrassed, I shrunk back in my chair and stared at the floor.

"If you need help with anything, there are services that can..." Julie tried to say.

My father immediately interrupted her. "I am helping her with everything," he stated.

My mother shook her head no, disagreeing with him. Julie helplessly looked at each of us, not quite sure how to handle this, not wanting to step on toes and make the situation worse.

My mother wrote a note on a piece of paper and showed it to Julie. "Lassen Hills."

My father said, "Oh, Ruth has an appointment at Lassen Hills Medical Center for further testing." He looked at another note my mother handed him, and added, "It's for a neurological evaluation."

"Oh, I didn't know that," I said, perking up. "I'd like to go with you."

"No, we don't want you to come. I will take her," he said simply.

"But I want to come," I responded. "I should be there. I want to help her and support her and ask the doctor questions and help you understand what he says. Mom, would you like me to go with you?"

My mother's eyes lit up and she nodded.

"*No!*" my father angrily yelled. "I forbid you to go. I will take her; we don't need or want your help."

Embarrassed, I glanced at Julie. Her eyebrows rose up in surprise.

"Dad, sometimes it helps just to have another person there to hear and understand what the doctor is saying, because it can be overwhelming. You don't have a medical background. I can assist with asking questions and also with understanding what is being said."

"*I said NO!*" he was now shouting, his face red. "You cannot go, you are not needed. I will help her; we do not want you there." He looked back and forth at us, his face defiant and angry.

Helplessly, I looked at Julie, who cleared her throat. "I think this should be Ruth's decision," she suggested, looking at my mother.

My mother looked stricken, uncomfortable with being on the spot, and she then withdrew into herself, refusing to answer any more questions. We let it go, we thanked Julie for coming, and we said good-bye, showing her to the door.

After Julie left, my mother started crying and shrieking. "Mom, what is it?" She did not respond.

I tried over and over to talk to her, but there was no response. She either stared straight ahead, cried, or shrieked. I reached for her to hold her, but she pulled away. After a short while, I finally left and went home.

Feeling heartsick and helpless, I worried about my mom all week. I wanted to go with her to the medical center so badly. I knew I could be of assistance, even if just for moral support.

8

A NEW DIAGNOSIS

The phone rang a few weeks later. "We've decided to let you come with us to your mother's appointment at Lassen Hills Medical Center," my father told me in a quiet voice.

Relieved, I let out my breath in a whoosh. "Great, thank you," I told my father. "I really want to help. I will start making a list of questions to ask the doctor."

"Good," my father said. "Because I don't know what to ask."

"I know," I answered. "That's why I need to be there."

I wrote down the location, date and time of the appointment, and I thanked him. And then I started writing a list of questions to ask the doctor.

A few days after that, my father called me back. "Your mother fell again," he said without even saying hello.

"What happened? Is she okay?"

"She hit her head on the floor and needed stitches."

"What? Where is she?" Fear rose in me sharply.

"She's home, she's fine, she's sleeping now." His voice sounded casual, like this was no big deal.

"I'll come visit tomorrow," I said.

The next day was cloudy, and there was a lot of traffic. It seemed to take forever to drive to their house, and that did not help the feeling of anxiety that was growing in my gut.

When I got to their house, I rushed in as soon as the door was answered. I found her sitting on the couch in the den, and I noticed that she had a bandage across her forehead.

"Mom, what happened?"

She got paper and wrote down a couple words. "I fell."

"How?"

"I was doing my volunteer work at the hospital. I was sitting on a stool with wheels. The stool slid out from under me."

"How awful! Are you okay?"

She scribbled some more. "I was already in the hospital, so they took care of me right away."

"How scary for you! I'm glad it wasn't worse than that."

"The hospital told me they no longer want me doing volunteer work there. Since I can't speak, and now that I fell, they said they don't need me anymore."

"Oh, I am so sorry, Mom!" She looked at me with sad eyes. "Mom, you know I've always been impressed with you for doing volunteer work for so many years, even into your seventies. It's amazing what you've done. Maybe it's time to rest and take care of yourself now. This might be a good thing — you'll be safer at home." She slowly nodded. It didn't look like she really agreed with me, but she nodded anyway.

"Mom, how did you fall? Were your legs feeling weak?"

She wrote some more. "No, the chair scooted out from under me."

I looked at her, not sure that I believed her. Maybe if her legs were stronger, she would have caught herself when she lost her balance or when the chair slid. Maybe her legs were getting weaker.

Then it struck me that if she was falling and her legs were weak, a simple cane would not be good enough, it would be too unstable. Julie, the case manager, had suggested to me that maybe she needed a quad cane, one of those canes with four little legs at the bottom, which are more stable. But now I started thinking that she may even need a walker at this time. But remembering my father's enraged reaction to the original pink cane, I was afraid to even bring that up.

"Is everything else okay?" I asked her.

She grabbed another piece of paper and wrote. "I want the bars that fit around a toilet to help me get up and down from the seat easier."

"Okay," I said, "we'll get that for you." To me, that was confirmation that her legs were getting weaker.

There was a medical supply store not very far away, and we decided to drive over and see what they had. We piled in my father's car and drove over there. However, when we arrived, we saw that the store was already closed for the day.

"I'll go back next week and get it," she wrote.

I was now convinced that her legs were definitely getting weaker and that she either didn't realize it or she didn't want to acknowledge it. Maybe admitting that her legs were getting weaker would mean admitting that more of her body was involved in the progression of the disease. Or maybe she was afraid of my father's reaction if she admitted that.

I decided to bring all of this up to the doctor at Lassen Hills when we went, and I added it to my list of questions to ask.

I had not yet discussed this with my parents, but I had also decided to bring a form for the doctor to sign so that my mother could get handicapped parking, since she was walking slower and falling more. I did not know how my parents would receive that, but this was a safety issue and I thought it was important.

I was trying very hard to make every step non-threatening and to present it as *helpful* for her rather than *needed* by her. I believed that this would be easier for my mother to accept and also less likely to set off my father. But I never could be sure.

Traffic was horrible on the day of the appointment at Lassen Hills Medical Center in March. I thought I had left plenty of time to get there, but with the bumper-to-bumper, stop-and-go traffic, it took me much longer than I had expected. A light drizzle did not help, and I kept needing to use the windshield wipers. I was anxious and nervous the entire trip, and I was afraid I might not make it in time.

Realizing that I was running late, I quickly parked my car and ran to the hospital waiting room, out of breath, hoping I didn't miss the start of their doctor visit. No — they were still there, sitting and looking at magazines. It seemed that the doctor was running late, too, and I was relieved.

I looked at my mother. She was sitting calmly, thumbing through a magazine.

"Mom, I brought a form to get handicapped parking for you. The doctor will need to sign it. I figured that this would be good for you, since you are walking more slowly and need more support. Even if you don't need it right now, it's good to have. Is that okay?"

She nodded right away and I was glad. As it was, when she walked, she would hold onto whoever was there with her, and she walked very slowly.

"You don't have to use it all the time, but it is good to have for when you need it." She nodded again.

While we sat in the waiting room, my mom wrote me a note. "It's getting harder to chew."

I immediately felt knots in my stomach. I did not want to see or hear any additional indications that the disease was progressing.

"Oh no, so it's even harder for you to eat now." She nodded.

"Are you using your cane?" She shook her head no.

"Mom, you need to use the cane more often to stay safe, so you will be more stable and less likely to fall." She nodded, but I had the feeling that she would not use it very often, if at all.

We were finally called to see the doctor, and we slowly walked into the neurology clinic office. I noticed that my mother was walking stiffly, holding onto my father's arm. She seemed stable, but her limbs seemed to be very rigid.

A middle-aged man in a white physician's coat greeted us. "Hi, I'm Dr. Grayson. How are you doing? Come in." He smiled at us warmly. We knew he was a top-notch neurologist, specializing in motor neuron diseases such as ALS. He was highly recommended and was said to be one of the best in that field.

The examination he gave my mother was very thorough and took a long time. He isolated and tested numerous specific muscles for strength, giving her instructions to squeeze, push, pull, or whatever movement he wanted in order to test her strength. He then tested numerous neurological reflexes, tapping and prodding in various areas.

After much testing, he then looked at us. "Her muscle strength is good, she is strong in her limbs. Her arms, legs, hands, and feet show strength within a normal range. I find that her reflexes are brisk."

He then asked my mother a series of questions. "Do you find yourself laughing or crying a lot every day?" She said yes.

"Has your handwriting changed?" She said yes.

"Have you lost weight?" She said yes.

"How much?"

"Forty pounds," I told him.

"Is she still losing weight?"

"No, she's been stable for a while."

"I'm giving her a new diagnosis," he then said. "I think she has PLS, or primary lateral sclerosis. This is still in the ALS family, and it is also a motor neuron disease, but it fits her better. It's also more rare than ALS and we don't see it a lot. In addition, it has a much better prognosis. The good news is that PLS is rarely fatal." He waited a beat, and then continued. "It is still progressive, but it progresses much slower than ALS. Whereas ALS progresses very fast and aggressively, and is usually fatal within three years, PLS progresses slowly over decades, and she will not die from this."

"This isn't fatal?" I asked to make sure I heard him right.

"No," he answered. She should have a normal lifespan. With ALS," he continued, "the muscles atrophy and waste away. But with PLS, her muscles will just get more stiff or rigid, but they will not atrophy. But don't forget that it is still progressive, so she still could find that it's getting worse in terms of speaking, chewing, swallowing, and difficulty with walking, but it will take a long time."

"Wow — this is great news!" I said.

He then continued. "She does not have any problems breathing, her lungs are strong. And she does not show any signs of fasciculations." I was glad — no tremors or twitches.

I had another question. "What about a feeding tube? Does she need one?"

"Not at this time," he answered. "However, if she finds that she develops trouble swallowing and cannot keep her weight stable, then she will need a feeding tube. But for now, since she can still eat soft foods, she can still swallow okay, and her weight is stable, she does not need one now."

I then handed the doctor the DMV form for a permanent handicapped parking placard, ready to plead a case of why she needs it, but he simply took it and signed it right away, without hesitation.

I felt a smile come across my face, and I just wanted to clap my hands and dance. This was *not fatal!* That was amazing and so nice to hear. I looked at my parents' faces, and they looked happy and relieved as well. We felt like rejoicing.

When we got out of the doctor's office, it was lunchtime, and we decided to eat at a little coffee shop right next to the medical center.

We walked in, ordered three tuna sandwiches, and brought it all to a table in the corner by a window. My father grabbed lots of extra napkins for my mother, prepared to clean up any food or drool that might fall from her mouth as she ate. Our lunch was very upbeat, and we happily talked about how fortunate it was that it was PLS and not ALS, and that it was not fatal. We were ecstatic, and the tremendous amount of hope and relief we felt was palpable. My mother was able to eat most of her tuna sandwich, and we were happy. This was definitely a very good day!

As soon as I got home, I did some research and looked up PLS on the Internet.

What I found was very interesting and enlightening. Just as with ALS, symptoms usually begin in the legs, but it may also start in the arms and hands, or the tongue. As the doctor had told us, PLS progresses gradually over a number of years or even decades. It can sometimes be difficult to differentiate a slowly progressing form of ALS from PLS. An accurate diagnosis of PLS is often delayed because it is often mistaken for ALS.

Wow! What a relief that she had PLS and not ALS! Whew! I did a happy dance in our living room, and then I sent an e-mail to the extended family letting them all know the good news.

9

ANOTHER FALL

Toward the end of March, we went to another ALS support group meeting. Dustin and I got there early and saved seats. When my parents arrived, I noticed that my mother had a bandage on her face near her eyebrow.

"Mom, what happened," I asked, concern in my voice. "Did you fall again?"

"She fell," my father told me. My mother then lifted her pants legs. Her knees were bloodied and bruised, and the bandages did a poor job of hiding that.

"What happened?" I asked.

"I tripped getting out of the car," she wrote.

"But something is different. You never used to trip getting out of the car. Are you feeling weaker?"

She wrote, "Lost my balance."

I wasn't so sure. I knew that something was different, because she had gone years without falling at all, and now she was falling a lot. I doubted that she was using the cane at all. And other than insisting that she use the cane to help keep her safer, I wasn't certain what else to suggest.

Then the meeting started and we took our seats. This one dealt with meditation, being in the "now" moment, metaphysics, and finding the gift in the disease, rather than constantly being angry and depressed and asking "Why me?" When it was my mother's turn to share, she wrote down, "I'm still angry," and I shared that with the group. I knew that she was still fighting the disease and not accepting it. I could understand that, but I also knew that by staying angry and depressed, she was not moving forward through the grieving process. She was stuck. I told the group that it is hard for us to work through the process of dealing with her illness when she is still having such a hard time. Everyone in the group nodded along, understanding the feelings.

Then it was my father's turn to share. "I'm Ruth's caregiver," he said proudly. "I take care of her every need." To this, both my mother and I shook our heads no. "Now, I want you all to understand that Ruth does *not* have ALS. Everyone with ALS will die within two to three years. That means that all of you," and he paused and pointed to everyone in the group, "will die within two or three years. But Ruth does not have ALS, so she won't die, and that is wonderful." He then smiled happily at everyone, pleased with himself.

The group was silent in response, and I choked back a gasp, feeling mortified. I looked at my mother, and her eyes were opened wide in shock. I quickly looked at the floor, my face hot and flushed. How could he be that horribly cruel and profoundly insensitive to the rest of the group? How could he not realize what he was saying to them? He was just living in his own world. I couldn't wait to get out of there.

After what seemed like a long silence, but was probably only a few seconds, the next person started sharing, but I did not hear a word of what was said after that.

At the end of the meeting, I went to the leader of the group and to Julie, our case manager, and I apologized to them for what my father said. They told me not to worry about it. Then I turned around and saw that my parents had already left and hadn't even said good-bye. I slowly moved toward the door, feeling like there was a big, gaping hole in my gut.

I drove out to visit my mother in early April. I saw that she was still not using the cane, but at least she had not fallen now in a few weeks. She was having good days and bad days, and this seemed to be one of the bad days, as she was crying when I got there.

The past few times I was there, I had been noticing that she got very emotional at times, crying over almost nothing. I wasn't sure what was underneath that, but I remembered that crying and being overly emotional were symptoms of the illness.

"Mom, tell me what's wrong. Talk to me."

She wrote, "I'm thinking about getting a feeding tube."

"Really? Why?"

"It takes me too long to eat. When we go out, I'm still on my soup, and Dad is already finished with his entire meal."

"Are you having trouble chewing or swallowing?"

"I can still eat soft foods and swallow okay, but I cannot chew, and it takes a long time to eat."

"Let's ask the support group about this the next time we go, okay?" She nodded.

I sat with her for a while, rubbing her back, while she closed her eyes.

At the end of April, we went to another ALS support group meeting. The topic was assistive devices, such as canes and walkers. When it was our turn to speak, I asked about feeding tubes. They said that one of the signs that you need a feeding tube is that it takes too long to eat. However, the two other people there with bulbar ALS, who also could not speak and could not eat, were not on feeding tubes. One of those men said that he put all his foods into a blender and drank it all. The other one said that it took him three hours to eat one plate of food, and that a few months earlier he had choked and aspirated his own saliva and then had pneumonia. I was surprised that neither of those men had a feeding tube; it sure sounded to me like they needed one.

I figured as long as my mother could still swallow and not choke, and was not losing more weight, she would be okay without a feeding tube. I was concerned that she might not be getting enough nutrition, but I knew that I would have to leave it up to her to decide when it was right for her.

After we got back to my parents' house, my mother started crying. "What's wrong?"

She wrote, "My bridge group dropped me."

I knew that she had been playing bridge with a group of three other women for years, and she had always enjoyed playing bridge.

"What happened? What did they say?"

She wrote, "They told me they no longer needed me." And she started crying harder.

"Oh Mom, I'm sorry," I said.

She wrote more. "I think they dropped me because I can't talk and contribute to their conversations. I write things down and give it to them to read, but the conversation has moved on by then." She blew her nose and then continued writing. "I think they dropped me because it is too disruptive and too much trouble to have me there."

Then she wrote more. "I still walk with my neighbor. I'm slower, but I still walk."

"I'm glad you're walking. Just go slow and be careful. Don't worry about the things you *can't* do anymore. Focus on and enjoy what you still *can* do. Find things that bring you pleasure and that you can do easily, and enjoy those." She nodded.

Over the next two weeks, I sent my mother a few greeting cards and e-mails letting her know that I was thinking of her. I reminded her several times to find and enjoy whatever she could still do that made her happy.

In early May, we visited my parents again. "I need to have cataract surgery," she wrote.

"Really? Do you have trouble seeing?"

"I don't see well up close."

"Are you scared of the surgery?"

She shook her head no.

"Do you need help getting to the surgery and back?"

She shook her head no and pointed to my father.

"Dad will take you?" She nodded.

"Mom, please e-mail me how you are doing. I don't trust what Dad says on the phone, he always says you are fine. I don't believe him, so I never know how you are really doing. I want to hear it from you how you are doing, so I'll know the truth. So e-mail me, okay?"

She just looked at me and did not respond. I knew I was getting fewer e-mails from her, and that it was probably getting more difficult for her to type and work the computer easily. So I thought I would not push too hard.

10

MORE DIFFICULTIES

Dustin and I went to visit my mom in May for Mother's Day. It was a warm, sunny day — one in which we desperately needed sunglasses against the intense brightness of the sun. Traffic was light and we made good time getting there.

My parents answered the front door. My mother was dressed all in pink, except for her standard brown sandals and white socks.

"Mom, how are you feeling?" She just stared and did not respond.

"Are you okay?" No response.

We moved into the den and sat down.

"Mom, I love you," I said simply. She looked at me, but she did not respond.

"Are you eating okay?"

She wrote, "It's getting harder to eat."

Then she added, "Dad still asks me what's for dinner."

"You mean he still expects you to cook for him?" She nodded her head yes.

"Dad," I asked him, "do you still ask Mom to cook you dinner?"

"Of course. She cooks dinner. I don't cook." He looked at me like this should have been understood.

"Mom, what do you cook for him?"

She wrote down, "Soup and frozen dinners."

"Dad, could you help her with making some of the dinners? Mom can't even eat."

He looked back and forth between my mother and me and said nothing.

"Dad, Mom will show you how to heat up the frozen dinners in the microwave. It's easy; it's just pushing a few buttons. And you could heat up a can of soup on the stove. That's easy too, and that would really help her."

He hesitated, then answered, "Okay, if she needs me to help, I'll help her." But I wasn't sure if he would follow through with that. I hoped that I was wrong, and that he would see how easy it was and would start helping her with that. But I knew that it would really be up to my mother to stop cooking for him so that he would need to do it himself.

In the evening, we all went out to dinner. It was still warm out, and we did not need coats. We went to a casual all-you-can-eat place where you had to serve yourself. Dustin and I went through the line and piled our plates high. My father helped my mother, and she came back to the table with soup and soft foods. But this time I noticed that she was struggling with even the soft foods. I saw her try to get the spoon in her mouth with jerky movements, and I watched as half of the food ran down her chin and all over her blouse. She leaned closer to the table and tried again. This time, food ran out of her mouth and fell on the table.

And she also had food stuck on her chin. Then I saw drool running out of her mouth and into her bowl of soup. When she noticed that, she started crying. Time seemed to stand still. Amid the loud bustle and conversations swirling around us in the restaurant, I watched my mother crying, drooling, and dripping food all over herself and the table. *This is the last time we eat out in a restaurant,* I thought.

After we returned to their house after dinner, my father looked at me happily. "I bought tickets to take your mother to a dinner dance," he said smiling.

"What?" I asked, dumbfounded at his state of denial.

"It's a dinner dance, it will be fun. There will be a nice dinner and dancing."

"Dad, Mom can't do that. She can't eat and she can't dance."

"She's fine. That's what we like to do. She can eat and she can dance."

"No, she can't. She's sick. How could you do this?" I looked at my mother. "Mom, do you want to go?" She looked back at me blankly.

"Mom, you don't have to go. You have the right to say no. Let him find another date to go with." My mother immediately smiled at that, and a strangled laugh came out of her. She looked at my father hopefully.

But he would not back down. "No, your mother wants to go. She'll be fine. We're going."

My mother's eyes dropped and the smile left her face. How could he not see this? How could he be so inappropriate, insensitive, and blind? How could he still be that much in denial? How could he not think about her needs and her limitations?

But I knew that this was typical of him, to not really think about anyone else's needs. The idea of a night out dining and dancing was so absurd. But again, I could not force the issue. This was between them. If my mother didn't want to go, she would have to tell him herself. I didn't want to start another fight, so I kept my mouth shut at that point, thinking I had already said enough.

Later that week, my mother e-mailed me that she lost more weight.

"Oh no," I e-mailed her back. "How are you feeling? And are you still going to that dinner dance?"

"I'm fine," she answered. "The dinner dance is here in the retirement community. Dad really wants to go. I don't have to eat or dance. I can just sit. It will be okay."

I then did research on a feeding tube to see what was involved. I discovered that it is a tube that would start from outside her abdomen, a little to one side, and would go directly into her stomach. A special formula of nutrients would be poured into the tube and would flow into her stomach. She would still be able to eat or drink a little by mouth, if she wanted to. But she would get most of her life-sustaining nutrition through the tube. The apparatus would have to be cleaned out after every meal to prevent growth of bacteria. So I knew there would be some maintenance involved with it. I was not sure that she was ready for this yet.

At the end of May, we went to another ALS support group meeting. This time, a guest speaker told us that people with ALS moved at a different speed than other people, and that that's okay. All of us, including the ALS patients, need to accept the fact and let it be okay to operate at a slower speed. She said that most people rush around and are too busy and then pay money to go to a seminar to learn how to slow down — and here we were learning it for free. There were chuckles all around. She talked about ways of slowing down and calming down so that we would not be stressed out and only focused on the disease. The information was helpful and the meeting felt supportive.

Afterward, I asked my mother, "Would you consider getting a walker? Look at that one," I said, pointing to a woman near the wall. "That one has a seat so you could sit down if you got tired. We can find one with a basket, too."

She wrote on a piece of paper and handed it to me. "I don't need one."

I didn't know if she just wanted to avoid another confrontation with my father, or if this was really how she felt. But either way, I knew I couldn't force it on her. It had to be up to her to decide when and if she needed more support. I decided to not press it further at that time.

"Are you using the handicapped parking?"

My mother nodded. "Good," I said. "That should help."

"Yes, it does help," my father added. "We use it everywhere we go now."

After the meeting, we drove back to my parents' house. My mother had bought the bars that fit around her toilet, and Dustin got busy installing them. With the extra support, she would be able to lift herself up more easily. When he was done, we brought my mother into the bathroom. She looked at the new bars and nodded.

It felt good to be able to do something to help her.

It was early June when I went back to visit my parents. This time I planned to really talk to my mother and make a strong connection. I wanted to let her know how much I loved her, and let her know how much I wanted to help her. And I hoped to get her to tell me how she was really feeling and dealing with everything.

When my father answered the door, I could hear my mother crying in the background.

"What's wrong with Mom? What happened?"

"I don't know," he stated simply.

My mother was sitting in the den on her favorite end of the old couch.

"Arrzzzghjjjzzz," she shrieked.

"Mom, what is it?" I asked. She did not respond.

"Write it down," I suggested.

She waved me off and started crying. I sat with her a few minutes and watched her cry.

"Mom, I love you," I said. There was no response. "Mom, I know this is hard for you. I want to help you. But we can't help you if we don't know what you need."

She seemed to calm down and stop crying, but there still was no other response.

"Do you need more help in the house? Should we get someone in to help you?" She shook her head no.

"Do you want me to come over more often? I can come every weekend and take you shopping or help you. Would you like that?" She shook her head no.

"You need someone to lean on emotionally, don't you," I said, and I felt tears stinging my own eyes.

I knew that my father could help her on a daily basis with physical tasks, but my mother desperately needed emotional support. I felt that my mother had spent her entire life helping others, trying to care for and please others. Now it was her turn. I asked her again if I could come every week, but the answer was still no.

I thought of something else. "How about if I call you on the phone and ask you yes-or-no questions, and you can grunt once for yes and twice for no, so I'd know your answer. Would you do that? Then we could talk more often." She shook her head no.

"Are you at least using the address labels I made for you? Does that help?" She shook her head no.

"Would you like to go for therapy? To talk to someone?" She shook her head no.

I knew that it was difficult to help her when she did not want it. Was it her pride? Did she want to still feel independent and capable? Or did she not want to bother anyone else? It broke my heart. I could see that she was suffering, yet I didn't know how to reach her.

I felt the weariness of the day seeping into my bones. I stopped pushing, and we talked about lighter topics for the rest of the day. Everyone relaxed more and my mother didn't cry again. But I knew that she was having a hard time.

I sent her e-mails almost daily that week, telling her how much I loved her and that I was in this with her, that she was not alone. I kept reminding her that she was not her body and not her disease, that she was still the same amazing and wonderful person that she always was and always would be. I let her know that I always liked spending time with her and hearing what she had to say, and that I was here for her.

I did not receive any response.

11

Club Med

I went back to visit them a week later. My mother was sitting in her favorite spot on the den couch, and I could tell that she had been crying recently.

"Mom, tell me what's wrong."

She wrote, "Dad leaves me alone all day and ignores me."

I saw my father in the kitchen reading a newspaper. "Dad, do you leave Mom alone all day and ignore her?"

"She's fine. She does her thing and I do my thing. She doesn't need me to sit with her all day."

My mother wrote, "He won't help me with the laundry or paying bills or washing pots."

"Dad, do you help Mom with the laundry?"

"No, she can do the laundry herself."

"Dad, she needs help with that. It's too difficult for her."

"She's fine, she can manage. She can do the laundry. That's her job, I don't do laundry."

"So you won't help her with that at all?"

"That's right, I won't do the laundry." He started to turn away and go back to his newspaper, as though the issue was resolved.

"What about paying the bills?"

He looked up at me. "Your mother pays the bills."

"What about washing the pots?"

"I help her load the dishwasher, but she can wash the pots. That's her job."

"Dad, maybe she needs more help than that."

He did not answer. I looked at my mother helplessly, and she blankly stared back at me.

Then she started crying again. I knew she was overwhelmed by it all.

On top of that, I understood that my mother would have to tell him what she needed every time. She wanted him to notice it and help on his own, but that was not part of his nature. I offered my assistance to her when I was there on weekends, asking if there was anything she needed done. But I worked full time and could only visit on a Saturday or Sunday, so I was limited in what I could do.

But here was my father, honestly still thinking that he was doing a great job of taking care of her on a daily basis. I knew that neither of my parents was willing to change and it was not in my control.

"Mom, next week we're all flying to Florida to go to Club Med. Are you still feeling well enough to go?"

She nodded and wrote, "I'm okay. I want to go."

"Will you be able to eat okay?" She nodded yes, and I continued. "They will have a large buffet and they should have enough soft foods that you will be able to find things that you can eat." She nodded again.

This was a vacation we were all looking forward to — an extended-family reunion at Club Med, with all the food and recreational activities included. Quite a few members of our family from New York would be there, including my mother's two sisters, my brother and his wife, and some of my cousins. It would also be a celebration of my parents' 60th wedding anniversary, so it was a special occasion. We happily chatted about the upcoming vacation, what we would do there, and the relatives we would see.

I was filled with anticipation all week. On the day we were flying out, Dustin and I left extra time and got to the airport early. My parents were going to meet us at the gate, and we saved two seats for them. But we didn't see them. An hour went by, and they were still not there. Did something happen? Was there a problem? I hoped they did not have an accident. My husband and I bought some lunch to take on board with us. Finally, about ten minutes before boarding, my parents came to the gate.

"What happened?" I asked.

My mother handed me a note. "They didn't want to let us bring the Ensure liquid."

"But you need that to eat, that's your nutrition."

"Security did not want to accept it. We told them it was doctor's orders — that it is all I can eat. I even have a doctor's prescription showing my disease and that I need this, but they said no."

"So you couldn't bring it?"

"We argued with them, and they got a supervisor. The supervisor looked everything over and then approved it and let us keep it."

"Oh my God, I'm glad they finally let you take it. That is scary — they need to be better informed about these situations." My mother nodded.

Then we heard the announcement that our flight was boarding. We picked up our carry-on luggage, got in line, and boarded the plane. The weather was clear and the six-hour flight was restful but boring. I flipped through a few magazines and closed my eyes a few times, but did not doze off.

Once in Florida, we rented a car and drove to Club Med, about thirty minutes away. It felt warm and humid, and we watched the sun set as we drove. We checked into the hotel and walked around the grounds for a while. It was tropical and beautiful, with many trees, flowers, and open grassy areas. We saw two swimming pools and a lake where you could rent boats. We saw a sandy area with a volleyball net, a putting green, and paths leading through beautiful green trees. We also saw that there was a circus-trapeze area and a few play areas for children. There were a few bars and restaurants, and lots of benches and places to sit and relax.

With all the traveling and the change in time zones, we decided to not stay up very long. We went to bed early, looking forward to seeing the rest of the family the next day.

The next morning at breakfast, we met up with other family members. "Stu!" I called, when I saw my brother and his wife, Brenda. We all hugged. Then we saw my mother's two sisters, Fran and Ellen, and Ellen's husband Adam approaching us. More hugs all around. My parents then joined the group, and there were still more hugs, accompanied by lots of smiles and happy talk as we all excitedly greeted each other.

We entered the dining room, filled up our plates with eggs, bacon, potatoes, French toast, pancakes, and fruit, and we then found seats together at one large table. I noticed that my mom's plate had scrambled eggs, which would be easy for her to eat. Breakfast was filled with happy conversation, catching up with each other, and multiple trips for more food.

After breakfast, my mother stayed with her two sisters, and Dustin and I went exploring. The place was huge, and it was spectacularly beautiful. Warm, hazy, and humid, the air smelled sweet and fresh. We spent an hour walking around the grounds and then settled into Adirondack chairs near the lake. We sat, breathing in the warm humid air, inhaling deeply, and drifting with our own thoughts. After a while, we strolled through beautiful gardens, holding hands and talking, simply enjoying the grounds.

As we turned toward a child's shout, we saw a few of our cousins who had just arrived. They had squirming children in tow, who were pointing somewhere down the path. After a quick and happy greeting, we watched them hustle off to the kiddie area.

The whole family met at noon for lunch, and we easily filled up two tables. I was impressed with the variety of choices for lunch, and realized that no one was going to go hungry here.

After lunch, we couldn't wait to jump in the pool. We put on our bathing suits and quickly walked over to the pool area. Stu and Brenda were already there, and we waded into the warm water. By the time we had swum a few laps, more of our family had arrived, including my parents, Fran, Ellen, Adam, and a few of my cousins. My cousins joined us in the pool, and we were happily swimming, splashing, and laughing. What a joy it was to see everyone!

After about an hour, something got my attention, and I saw Stu, Ellen, Adam, and Fran swarming around my mother by the lounge chairs near the edge of the pool. Feeling alarmed, I quickly got out of the pool and went over to them.

"What happened?" I immediately looked at my mother, as Adam was helping her to sit in one of the chairs.

"Ruthie fell," Ellen said. "The ground was wet, and she tripped over a lounge chair leg. But she didn't fall all the way down. Adam caught her."

I could see that my mother was a little scared and embarrassed, but we could tell she was fine, just a little shaken up.

"Mom, walk slowly," I said. "Be careful." She nodded.

Hesitating, I glanced back and forth from my mother to Ellen. "Don't worry Lynn," Ellen said when she saw my face. "I'll sit with her, she'll be okay."

Feeling a bit relieved, I rejoined Dustin and my cousins in the pool. After a few more hours of swimming, splashing, and laughing, we all went back to our rooms to change for dinner.

The meals were all buffet style, and there were various food stations arranged around a large room. Our entire family was assigned to one large table, so we all were able to sit together for dinner. After filling up my plate with assorted food, I went back to our table. I saw my mother coming back also, holding a plate. She had it filled with mashed potatoes and steak.

"Mom, you can't eat steak. That's not soft food."

She ignored me and started eating the mashed potatoes. I glanced at her plate throughout the meal and saw that she ate the soft food but did not touch the steak. I thought that either it was an old habit to get the steak that she used to love, or she was filled with hope and longing. Or maybe she felt transported back in time with her sisters, and she forgot she wouldn't be able to eat that. When she was done, she pushed her plate away, with the steak untouched.

After dinner, Fran pulled me aside to talk to me. "I was helping Ruthie get dressed after swimming," she told me. "She couldn't figure out what to wear and how to get dressed. She needed help. Eric wouldn't help her. He got dressed and left the room, leaving her there alone. And her bathing suit was still in the sink, not rinsed out. It's too hard for her to rinse it; she needs help with that. Your father is not really helping her, and I feel bad for her."

I thanked Fran for telling me, and I walked up ahead to catch up to my father. "Dad," I said, "Mom needs help with getting dressed."

"No she doesn't, she can get dressed by herself," he stated simply.

"She needs more help than you think. You just assume she's fine, but you need to slow down and check with her and see if she needs help."

"She doesn't need help," he repeated.

"And her bathing suit is not rinsed out. She needs assistance with that, too."

"I'm not going to rinse out her bathing suit, that's hers. She can do it."

"It's too hard for her by herself, she's not as strong as she used to be."

"I rinsed out mine, and she can rinse out hers. I'm not going to do hers."

"You're not going to help? Are you *refusing* to help her?" I shouted, my voice louder than I wanted it to be.

Fran hurriedly came over to me. "Shhhh," she whispered, "don't push it. Don't make it worse."

"No, someone needs to tell him. He shouldn't get away with this," I answered quickly, feeling the adrenaline pulsing in my body.

"Leave him alone," she said. "Let it go."

"No!" I said and went back to my father, confronting him. "Are you refusing to rinse out Mom's bathing suit?"

He suddenly got enraged. He turned to me, his face red and furious. I saw his right hand, clenched into a fist, come up to strike me, and he started lunging at me.

My stomach constricted in fear and shock, and I darted to the side so that he couldn't reach me. Gasping, I ran back to my room, Dustin closely following.

Once in my room, I felt my body convulse with choking sobs, and I turned toward my husband. "I hate him!" Dustin handed me a tissue. "I really hate him! I want nothing more to do with him!" My eyes squeezed shut and my body shook as I sobbed.

My husband let me rant and cry for a while, and we stayed in the room for the rest of that evening.

The next few days went fast. We got together often with other family members, swimming, laughing, talking, and walking around, but I kept a big distance from my father. My mother's two sisters stayed with her throughout each day, so I knew she was in good hands, and I didn't have to worry about her. Dustin and I spent time catching up with my brother and my cousins. We rented paddleboats and rowboats and went out on the smooth, clear lake. We swam every day in the large pool, and then spent time walking, exploring, and taking advantage of everything that was available to do.

After a few days, my muscles felt sore from all the exercise, my sides ached from laughing so much, and my spirit felt refreshed and upbeat. I was still staying away from my father.

On our last day, everyone was leaving at different times, depending on varying schedules and airline flights. My parents were going with Fran up to her house in New York for another week, so in the late morning, after saying our good-byes, Dustin and I packed up and drove to the airport by ourselves.

12

SACRAMENTO

Julie contacted my mother in July and suggested that she get additional assistance. She said that in her judgment, my mother needed outside help — someone who would come into their home a few days a week, a few hours at a time, to assist her with various tasks.

Julie then called me with the warning that if my father refused this assistance for my mother and neglected her, we would have to call adult protective services.

At hearing those words, I felt my gut clench. I knew that my mother did not want outside help coming into her house. I wasn't sure that we should be forcing something like that on them, and it seemed a bit extreme to me. My gut said not to press the issue just yet.

About a week later, toward the end of July, my parents, Dustin, and I traveled to northern California to visit my brother and his wife for a few days. My parents met us at our house and we drove together to the airport. Once our bags were checked, we bought lunch and sat down at a table to eat. As I hungrily ate my lunch, I saw that my mother was having a hard time eating her salad, which was topped with a scoop of tuna. We watched her eat slowly, with very little getting into her mouth, and we noticed that drool was dripping into her remaining salad. As the time went by, I glanced at my watch multiple times and realized that she was eating too slowly. Our flight would be leaving shortly, and we had been sitting there for almost an hour.

"Mom, we need to get going to make our flight," I gently said.

My mother looked at me, looked at her almost-full bowl of food, and started crying. My heart ached. She then pushed her food toward me and asked if I wanted any. I was actually still hungry and appreciated her loving gesture, but I knew that she had been drooling into her food.

"No, thanks," I said, and attempted to smile at her. I then stood up and took her food to throw it out. We then hurried to the gate to make the flight.

Once our flight landed in Sacramento, we rented a car and set out for Stu and Brenda's house. It was over an hour's drive through beautiful, lush green scenery that alternated between farmland and forest. We finally arrived at their home, which sat in the midst of a grove of trees, and we pulled into a dirt parking space across from their house. Their large home sat on a few acres and had spectacular views of the surrounding forest. There was also a small guest house for visitors, and we brought our suitcases in there and settled in.

Stu and Brenda welcomed us warmly, giving us snacks and cold beverages while asking about our flight.

Stu then showed us around the property. They lived at the top of a hill, surrounded by acres of trees and natural forest. As we were walking down a path and being careful where we were stepping, Stu suddenly stopped and pointed. We followed his gaze and noticed a small deer, its tail twitching. It looked back at us for a few moments, lowered its head back down in the leaves, and then looked up and scampered off. We let out our collectively held breath and smiled at each other. As we continued walking, we found ourselves breathing deeply, inhaling the woods-and-dirt scented air, noticing how much more clear and energized we felt.

Brenda was a great cook and her food was delicious. We found that since the rest of us ate faster than my mother, if we cleared the plates or moved on to dessert too soon, my mother would get agitated and upset. But if we sat there and did not clear the plates or move on to dessert right away, then my mom did not feel rushed. She was able to take her time and eat slowly, as there was no pressure on her. We then consciously slowed down and paced ourselves so she would feel more comfortable.

We fell into a leisurely, relaxed tempo, eating outside on the patio, walking through the woods, talking, laughing, and simply unwinding. With no set deadlines, my mother was able to relax and move at her own speed without rushing, and she seemed much calmer and happier. The three days went by fast.

After packing and saying our good-byes, we flew back to Los Angeles with my parents, and drove back to our house. We hugged them good-bye, and they then made their way back to their house.

Later that week, my mother went to a speech therapist for an evaluation. Although it was obvious that she could not speak, this was necessary in order to get a prescription for a communication device that she could type on and which would speak for her. So she went to the speech therapist, had the evaluation, and got the prescription. Now she would be able to get the device. I was glad — the more she could get to assist her, the better.

When I next visited my mother, she handed me a note. "I'm having trouble breathing."

"What? How? What's wrong?"

"After meals or after walking, it gets hard to breathe."

I felt my stomach knot up, realizing that her lungs were getting weaker.

She handed me another note. "I'm looking into a BiPAP machine to assist me." Then her hand shook and she started crying.

"Oh my God," I said.

Maybe she would feel better once she started using the breathing apparatus, as she would get more oxygen to her body and then possibly feel stronger.

"Mom, I think that will help you. I know the machine will be an adjustment, but it will be good for you, you will feel better." She looked at me with sad eyes.

She then wrote some more. "I am planning on having someone come in to help me."

"That is great, Mom. You need help. You are doing too much on your own. And you are too isolated. It will be nice to have someone here for a little companionship, too."

She nodded and closed her eyes.

"Look, Mom — I made some flash cards to help you when you go to the store. Here's a card that says, 'paper please.' This is for when you go to the supermarket. This one says, 'May I please have a rain check,' for when a store is out of something — you can just show them this and point to the item. And here's one that says, 'stamps please,' for when you go to the post office."

She nodded and took the cards. I didn't know if she would use them, but I hoped they would help her so she would not have to struggle so hard to communicate when she needed to take care of daily tasks.

My father called me later that month. "We are going to take a trip to Germany," he said.

"What? That's not a good idea," I told him.

"We want to visit Germany," he repeated, like nothing was wrong.

"That will be too much for Mom. She can't walk much, she keeps falling, and she can't eat. What if she needs a doctor?"

"She's fine, there's no problem, and we want to travel," he said as though it was a trip to the local store.

"What if she gets injured in a foreign country? What will you do? How is she going to keep up with a tour group? What will she eat? You are not being realistic. This is too much for her."

"She's fine, we'll be fine. Everything's okay. We're going to Germany."

"Dad, she had trouble at Club Med in Florida, just a couple months ago. She fell there, remember? She moved slowly, and it was hard for her to eat. It was difficult for her here in her own country, surrounded by family."

"She was fine, there was no problem."

He was dismissing everything I said, like he usually did. However, going to Germany would put my mother in danger. But as the conversation would most likely escalate and start a fight, I realized that I had to let it go, at least for now. Maybe he would be more rational another time and we could discuss it then.

I then sent an e-mail to my mother, addressing all my concerns about their trip to Germany, and how I felt it was a bad idea. I explained that my father was not taking her needs into account, and that she had the right to say no. She did not respond.

About a week later, my mother e-mailed me that maybe it would be okay to go to Germany, that she's feeling a little better, and that she should be fine.

I immediately wrote her back and explained that I thought she was overestimating her abilities and not being honest about her condition. I asked her how she was going to keep up with a tour group walking fast in a foreign country. I asked her how she was going to eat fast during their quick meal breaks, where the choice of food may be limited.

About a week after that, she sent me an e-mail saying that they decided not to go to Germany, that she would not be able to get up early on a tour and rush through her meals to keep up with everyone. I let out an audible sigh of relief.

We went to the next ALS support group meeting on a Saturday in July. The guest speaker was a nutritionist. She spoke about types of foods that are more difficult to eat and types that are easier to eat. She then went into detail about how to make foods in general easier to eat. She also brought some information about feeding tubes.

"Mom, do you think you want a feeding tube yet?"

She shook her head no and wrote, "My weight is stable. I want the BiPAP machine for breathing first."

Oh, how my heart ached for her. What difficult issues she had to confront and make decisions about.

When the meeting was over, we went back to their house. Once there, she handed me another note. "I can still eat soft foods okay. I cannot drink thin liquids, I choke on that."

"But thicker liquids are okay?" I asked her.

She nodded and wrote, "Juice nectars and apple sauce I can get down okay."

Once I got home, I did research on BiPAP machines. I found that it is a device that has a mask that one would wear, and it would push oxygen into one's lungs, expanding the lungs, and then it would allow the patient to release the air on her own. So if someone was having trouble getting enough oxygen, especially if their lungs were weak and they could not take a deep breath, this machine would force the air in so that they would get deep breaths, and that would help to expand the lungs so that they did not atrophy and get weaker. It looked like it might be uncomfortable, and I hoped my mother would have an easy time adjusting to it.

A nurse went to see my mom that week with the BiPAP machine and helped set it up for her. The nurse said that my mother should use it a few times a day, for just ten to fifteen minutes at a time, at least in the beginning. However, the nurse said that if her lungs continued to get weaker, it was possible that she may need it more and more often, and possibly eventually even need a ventilator to continually breathe for her. But that would be somewhere down the road, and we didn't have to worry about that yet — one scary, overwhelming step at a time. For now, she was to just use it a few times a day and get used to it.

13

SIGNS OF CONFUSION

My next visit to my mother was on a hot, sweaty day, and I was glad my parents had put on their air conditioning. As soon as I got there, my mother handed me a note, "My doctor gave me a prescription for a walker."

"A walker? Are you going to get one?"

"Yes, I'll look for one," she wrote.

"Good — whatever will help keep you safe is good. Do you want me to come with you to look for one?" She shook her head no, and I decided not to press it.

She said that she liked holding on to a shopping cart when she went shopping, so she knew a walker would be helpful.

After I got home, I called Stu. My brother had flown down and visited my parents about a week earlier, and I wanted to share with him the latest.

"Stu," I said after he answered the phone, "I just saw Mom. She is going to get a walker."

"What?" he answered, surprise in his voice. "She told me she didn't want one when I was there last week."

"Did she have the doctor's prescription at that time? She showed that to me and said she was going to get one."

"Yes, she showed me the prescription too, but she told me no, she definitely did not want one and would not get one."

"I wonder if she changed her mind. Or if she's confused."

"She didn't seem confused to me," he said, but he sounded unsure.

"Was she okay otherwise?"

"Well, she cried a lot. And she also wrote a note that made no sense, and I couldn't figure out what she was saying."

"Maybe she did get confused. Let's not push too hard for things with her right now. Maybe this needs to be up to her," I told him.

And for now, I thought that maybe she simply needed more compassion and understanding. Feeling loved and supported could go a long way.

In early August, on another hot, blustery day, I went to my parents' house, planning to ask my mother about the walker, about the BiPAP machine, and about the communication device. I also wanted to really talk to her and have a heartfelt conversation about how she was feeling.

As I approached their front door, I could hear shrieking inside, and my stomach fell. Either something was wrong or she was having a bad day. Reluctantly, I pushed the doorbell and listened to it chime inside the house. It took a while for the door to open. When my father finally opened it, I could hear my mother crying in the background, and my father stood there, looking frazzled.

"Hi, Dad, how is Mom? What's wrong?"

"I don't know. She won't tell me," he said, and I could hear the frustration in his voice.

I walked into the den, and saw my mother sitting on her end of the old brown couch, crying.

"Hi, Mom. How are you feeling? What's wrong?"

She ignored me and continued crying, a damp and crumpled tissue clutched in her left hand.

"Mom?" I tried again.

She shrieked and pointed toward the opposite wall.

"What is it? What do you want?"

She shrieked again and pointed. I looked toward where she was pointing, but I saw nothing. I looked helplessly at my father. "What does she want?"

"I have no idea. She won't tell me," my father said, as he walked out of the room.

I felt anxiety bubbling up in my gut. "Mom, write it down," I told her.

She shrieked some more and then dissolved into loud sobs. I had no idea what to do. I handed her more tissues and a pad of paper and a pen, but she ignored all of that.

Feeling a choking sense of anxiety rising up from my gut, I looked at my mom. I did not want to see her like this, but I could not look away. With trembling hands, I reached toward her to gently hold her and tell her I loved her, but she sharply pulled back, and pointed toward the other side of the room and shrieked again. What was wrong? What did she want? She shrieked again, pointing with agitation and intensity. I had no idea what she wanted, and I felt a knot in my throat.

"The chair? The door? The wall? Is it in this room?" I asked, hoping for a response, any clue of what she wanted.

She shrieked louder, and then she looked at me. I had no idea what she wanted. Feeling helpless, I looked away.

My mother broke down into wails, grabbing at some extra tissues, and I went looking for my father.

"Do you have any idea what she wants?" I asked him.

"No. I've asked her, I tried to get her to write it down, but she won't tell me."

I could tell that he was upset. I knew that he wanted to help her, but he didn't know what to do. I did not know what to do either, and I felt helpless and unsettled.

In the den, my mother's wailing had softened into a whimpering. I tried a few more times to talk to her and get her to write something down, but she just ignored me.

About an hour later, she handed me a note. I kept looking at it, my stomach flipping. It was gibberish. I sat with her for a while, saying nothing.

After another hour, I decided it was time to leave. I drove back home, breaking down and sobbing in the car.

14

Trouble Breathing

About a week later, my mother finally had some outside help come to their house to assist her. The woman's name was Maria. Maria was there for only a few hours.

To this day, I'm not sure exactly what happened. According to my father, my mother asked Maria to take her to the store. Maria said she had no gas in her car and my father then fired her. According to Maria, she quit because the atmosphere was so tense in the house, my mother wouldn't write down why she was crying, my father was rude to Maria, and she would not work under those conditions. I also heard that my father then called up the agency and told them to tear up the contract.

I spoke to my mother about a week after that. She said that she did not want help coming to the house, she wanted her privacy and independence. So I figured I would not push it, and I thought the best thing we could do was to honor her wishes. She could always get outside help later if she changed her mind. I hoped that for now, my father's help would be enough.

My brother flew down toward the end of August and visited with my parents to see what was going on and how he could help. Stu asked her what she most wanted from my father, and she said for him to stop being so impatient with her. She said she often didn't get lunch because he would have lunch fast on his own and then forget about her.

My father explained that she often didn't know what she wanted to eat, and then he would simply get busy with other things. Stu then made up a menu for her, so she could just point to what she wanted for each meal. We hoped that would help, but I had my doubts, since she did not seem to be using any of the lists that we had previously given her.

I started realizing that everyone had such a different view of my mother, her illness, her capabilities, and what she needed or didn't need. Some people in my family thought she needed a lot of help, some people thought she needed occasional help, and some people, like me, thought she was getting by okay with help from her husband, and that she valued her privacy and independence more than outside help.

I knew that she had good days and bad days, so it would not be a simple one-size-fits-all answer. I was sure that there were some days when she needed help, and some days when she was fine without it. I realized that this was not as clear-cut as we would like, and one quick fix would not be suitable for all days. The "right" solution was still elusive.

One week later, Dustin and I went back to my parents for a visit. *Please let her be feeling good today,* I thought, as I rang the bell.

The door sprang open, and my father was standing there, smiling. "Come in," he said, and I went into the den.

My mother looked up at me from the book she was reading, then smiled and grunted a greeting. I loved seeing her smiling and doing a normal activity.

After talking for a few minutes, I looked at my mother. "Would you like to go to the T-shirt Factory today? We need some new sweatshirts."

Her face immediately lit up and her smile got bigger. She loved going shopping and this would be a real treat for her. She nodded happily and went to get her purse. She came back quickly, looking expectantly at us with bright eyes.

We piled into my father's car, and he drove us to the store in Oxnard, about twenty minutes away. It looked like one large warehouse room, with many rows of clothes and various other items like luggage, purses, and costume jewelry in the front of the store. My mother, husband, and I eagerly scampered off in search of various items, while my father found a chair near the entrance, where he sat down to wait for us. About thirty minutes later, our arms filled with bags of newly bought goodies, we got back in the car for the drive back to their house.

Feeling relaxed and happy, we talked with each other and shared what was happening in our lives. The entire afternoon was calm, peaceful, and fairly normal. We talked about everyday things and made fun of whatever we could, just like old times. It was thrilling to have such a regular, boring, happy day.

Just before we left, my mother handed me a note. "Thank you for helping me."

I read the note a few times and gave her a big hug.

We went to the next ALS support group meeting at the end of August. The guest speaker was a physical therapist who demonstrated various movements we could help the patients perform so that their muscles would stay more flexible and not get too stiff. It was interesting, I took a lot of notes, and the time passed quickly.

At the end of the meeting, when my parents started to leave the room, I tried to hug my mother, but she just moved away. I was not sure why, and I walked with my parents out to their car, unsure if I should try to hug her again. When they got to the car, I started to move toward them to say good-bye, but they ignored me, and I watched as my mother simply got into the car and shut the door. She sat facing forward, stiff and immobile, waiting to leave. She did not look at me or wave good-bye. It was painful to watch. Was she angry with me? Did I do something wrong? Was she not feeling well? I wanted so much to help her and reach out to her, and I felt shut out and helpless. I felt a deep sadness filling me. My gut ached, and I wanted to cry.

As I thought about it at home later that afternoon, I realized that I had been hoping that my mother and I would become closer through all this, and that we would bond and share this together and cry together. I longed for her to lean on me and confide in me more. But she kept shutting me out.

Overcome with frustration, helplessness, and heartache, I punched the couch pillows and felt tears roll down my cheeks. I hated ALS and PLS and all its related forms — what awful diseases!

On a cloudy and windy day in September, I drove out to my parents' house for a visit. *I hope she's feeling better today,* I thought, as I rang the bell.

Both my parents stood there as the door opened. My mother was attempting to smile, and I felt relieved. So far, so good.

"Mom, how are you doing?" She nodded that she was okay.

"How is the BiPAP machine? Are you using it?"

She smiled weakly and went to get it to show me. It had a mask that covered only her nose and a strap that was supposed to hold her jaw closed so that she would not breathe through her mouth. The machine would force air into her nose and into her lungs, and then she would exhale on her own.

"How often are you supposed to use this?"

She wrote down, "Once a day, for 4 hours at a time."

"Are you doing that?"

A funny laugh came out of her and she shook her head no. She wrote down, "Less than that, but at least I'm using it."

"Is it comfortable?" She shook her head no and then shrugged.

I smiled at her. "Well, try to keep using it as much as you can. This will help your lungs inflate fully and help them remain healthy and functional longer." She nodded, but I knew that she would use it for however long she wanted. I hoped she would at least use it every day.

She then brought over a black plastic machine that looked a little like a laptop. This was the machine that speaks for her — this one was called a Dynawrite. She could type in what she wanted to say, and it then would speak what she typed. She could also store phrases in memory, type in a code (the first two letters of the phrase and a space), and it would then automatically fill in the entire phrase and speak it. It seemed like it would be fairly easy for her to use.

I read through the instructions, we picked a female voice that was the easiest to understand, and I adjusted the volume. Then I entered all kinds of phrases for her such as, "I want to go to Vons," "I'm hungry, let's eat," and "Leave me alone." I also put some fun and silly ones in there. I was having fun programming these phrases in, and we were laughing. My mother was happy, and she pointed to my father and then had the machine clearly say, "You are a pain in the ass." She laughed and pointed and pressed "speak" again so that it repeated it over and over. I hadn't seen her so excited and happy in a long time.

15

A Feeding Tube

I received an e-mail from my mother in October. "I'm going for a feeding tube," she wrote. "I will spend one night in the hospital and come home the next day. Wish me luck."

I sent her back an e-mail and asked her why she was getting it now.

She wrote back, "I lost some more weight. I also started choking when trying to eat or drink."

I called up my father and asked him about it.

"She's going in on Thursday this week."

"Do you know if she's having general anesthesia for this?"

"She said she'll be sedated, but it will not be general anesthesia."

"Tell her good luck and I love her and I'll be thinking of her."

On Friday I called my father. "Is she home? Is everything okay?"

"They are keeping her another day."

"Why? Was there a problem?" I felt my stomach flip — I hoped there were no complications.

"They didn't say, they just want her there another day."

On Saturday I called back and asked if she was home yet.

"No, they said her hemoglobin was low, so they are keeping her one additional day. I'll be bringing her home tomorrow."

On Sunday afternoon, feeling overcome with worry, I called again. "Is Mom home?" I asked when my father answered the phone.

"Yes, she's home, she's fine."

"Is she in pain?" I asked, feeling relieved that she was home.

"No, she's not in any pain at all."

"Have you fed her through the tube?"

"Yes, it's easy. I fed her a few times already, and they gave me enough of the liquid food for four days."

"And then what? Where do you get more food?"

"I don't know."

"Call the nurse at the hospital and ask."

"Okay," he said. "I'll call."

The next weekend, I went to visit them. It was Saturday morning, and the sun was already bright and strong. When she opened the door, she was smiling, a weak and crooked smile, but it looked good and warmed my heart.

"Mom, how are you feeling? How is the feeding tube?"

She proudly pulled up her blouse and showed me. There was a small, thin tube sticking out of her abdomen, but it was not visible under her blouse, so no one would have known. She showed me the can of the nutritional drink that gets poured down the tube.

"Is it easy?" She nodded.

"Do you feel better?" She nodded. I felt relieved. I knew she would be getting better nutrition this way and she should be feeling stronger.

At lunch, we sat down at the kitchen table. My father got a can of the special liquid food for her, and he opened it. My mother sat in a chair by the wall and pulled up her blouse to expose the feeding tube. I watched as my father poured the liquid into a fat syringe and pushed the liquid into the tube. When the tube was filled up, he stopped pouring, waited for the liquid to go down, and then repeated the process. When the can was empty, he poured a half-cup of water into the tube to wash it all down and flush out the tube. Then he put my mother's medications into an envelope, grabbed a hammer, and got down on the floor. He pounded the envelope with the hammer over and over, smashing the pills into a pebbly powder. Rising from the floor, he poured the crushed tablets into the feeding tube, and then emptied another half-cup of water into the tube. My mother sat there calmly throughout the ordeal.

"Mom, do you feel anything? Do you feel it going in?"

She shook her head no.

"Wow, Dad, that's time consuming and a lot of effort!"

"It's easy, it's no big deal. I do this three or four times a day, every day," he said nonchalantly. I was impressed at how he dismissed his own efforts, especially seeing how much work was involved, and I knew this would be going on for a long time.

"Did you find out how to get more food?"

"Yes," my father answered. "They sent me a shipment of cans to last a month, and I can also get this at the local drugstore. So we'll be okay."

After lunch, my mother and I moved into the den and sat down, while my father sat down in the kitchen to read the newspaper.

My mother handed me a note. "Dad does not take care of me."

"But he's taking great care of you. Look at what he's doing with feeding you through the feeding tube. What else do you need?"

She wrote, "attention."

"I'm so sorry," I told her, reaching for her hand. "Everything would be easier for you if you had more emotional support at home. Without that, everything is harder, I know."

She nodded and a tear rolled down one cheek.

As I handed her a tissue, I noticed that her right arm was shaking — there was a clear, pronounced tremor and repetitive shaking of her right arm and hand.

"Mom, are you having trouble controlling your arm? Have you noticed your arm shaking?"

She started crying harder and nodded her head yes.

At that, my father walked into the den and loudly said, "No, she's not having any problem with her arm."

My mother's sobs grew louder.

"Dad, I've noticed it a few times within just the past two hours. You're living with her — don't you see it? Haven't you ever noticed this?"

I looked at her arm again — it was not shaking. Then it started again. It looked like a strong, pronounced spasm, with her muscles contracting on their own, or due to some nerve impulse, which is similar to the tremors caused by ALS that I had read about.

I swallowed hard. I knew this was another symptom of the progression of the disease. I felt so bad for my mother — she had enough to deal with, and this would make it even more difficult for her.

"Mom, tell the doctor about this the next time you see him, okay?" She nodded.

I looked at my father. "Dad, you really need to pay more attention to Mom. She needs you."

"I help her with everything she needs," my dad said quickly.

I knew he was helping her a lot, so I didn't want to come down too hard on him. And I also knew that he would never be good at helping my mother with her feelings. People are who they are and I knew we could not change him into someone else.

While I was there, I tried reaching out and talking more to my mother and asking her some questions. But her responses were conflicting. To many of my questions, she first nodded her head yes, then she shook her head no. Then she wrote down an incomplete answer that I asked her to clarify. She wrote another few words with incomplete information regarding something entirely different.

I didn't know if she misunderstood me or if she was having trouble expressing herself. Either way, the communication was not very good, and it seemed that something was confused somewhere in her brain. Feeling frustrated, I finally gave up asking her questions, and just kept telling her that I loved her and that I hoped she was feeling okay.

My brother flew down that week to spend a few days with my parents and see if he could help. He called me after he got back home.

"Mom does not want or need much help right now," Stu said. "She wants her privacy rather than someone in her house. They have arranged for their next-door neighbor to come over once a week for about two hours to make lunch and take her shopping. So that should help. And Dad promised to treat caregivers with more respect."

"That's good," I said.

"And I also spoke to the doctor," he added. "They have increased her dosage of her antidepressant, so hopefully she will be feeling better. But it could take a couple weeks to notice a difference."

"Okay," I said. "I hope that helps."

I went back to visit my mother in late October. She said she had some pain in her belly, and she thought my father was letting too much air into the syringe when he gives her the food. I talked to him and made sure he knew to be careful about not having air in the tube so that only liquid gets put into her stomach. He said okay, but I was not sure he understood.

My mother then wrote me a note. "I have a bill for you to pay from our checkbook."

"You want me to help you pay your bills?"

She nodded yes and handed me another note. "It's too much for me. The checkbook is a mess. I used to do it all. Now Dad does it but he messes it up."

"Okay, let me take a look at it."

She handed me her checkbook. I noticed right away that the entries were messy and out of order. Some entries were added to the total, but not all. It was very inconsistent.

"Do you have a bank statement to try to reconcile this to?"

She handed me their last bank statement. I started comparing the bank statement to the checkbook, thinking I could at least match up the entries. But after 40 minutes of trying to match things up, I realized there were entries in the checkbook that were not on the bank statement, and entries on the bank statement that were not entered in the checkbook. There were also duplicate entries in the checkbook, and the math was not done correctly — simple additions and subtractions were wrong. It was impossible to decipher and make it right.

"Mom, this is all messed up. Nothing makes sense."

She gave me a half smile and nodded. "Mom, Dad can't do this. Someone else has to do this for you if you can't do it. But it can't be Dad."

Then I heard heavy footsteps pounding into the den. "There is nothing wrong with my entries. Mine are all perfect. Your mother messed everything up."

"What? These entries are your handwriting."

"That's right, your mother ruined everything. It's all her fault."

My mother started to cry.

"Dad, you're not making sense. Mom took care of this for years and there wasn't a problem. Now it's too much for her, and you started doing it. But your entries don't make sense."

"My entries are perfect, there is nothing wrong with them."

"Dad, you have duplicate entries and missing entries. I can't reconcile this."

"Who asked you to? Get out of here, this is none of your business."

"Mom asked me to write one check for her and to look at the checkbook."

"How dare you try to take this over. I can do this, I don't need any help."

My mother stood up from the couch and started to try to say something. My father took one look at her, brusquely pushed her backward so that she fell back onto the couch, and he then took two menacing steps toward me. I saw his right hand rise and his fist clench, and I knew he was getting ready to hit me.

Gasping, I stepped back and looked at my mother. She had landed easily on the den couch, unhurt, but she looked shocked and startled.

"Mom, are you okay?" She just stared straight ahead and said nothing.

My father stood there poised, his fist still raised, ready to strike, anger pulsing in his red face.

"Get out of here!" he shouted at me.

"Mom, I'm sorry," I said to my mother, as I picked up my purse and keys. "I'll see you tomorrow."

I drove home, choked with anguish, gripping the wheel tightly, sobs filling the car. What did I do wrong? What could I have done differently? How could I help my mother when my father kept getting in the way and not letting me? What could I do?

16

HAPPY BIRTHDAY

The next day, I drove back there, my stomach in knots. I did not want to see my father at all. But I did not want to abandon my mother and leave her without any support. I felt that I had to put my mother's needs ahead of my own discomfort.

I had no idea if my father would still be angry and defiant or if he had calmed down. Afraid to even face him, I held back and stood on their porch a full minute before ringing the bell. I listened to the bell chime inside the house, half wishing that no one was home so I could just leave and say that I tried.

The door opened, and my father stood there. "Hi, welcome, come in," he said happily, like nothing was wrong and nothing bad had ever happened.

"I'm just feeding your mother," he added, as he went back to the kitchen. I followed him in there and saw my mother sitting in the chair by the wall. My father poured the nutritional drink into the syringe and down the feeding tube, while my mother sat there staring off into space.

I watched in silence as my father took care of her, carefully feeding her, and then pouring water down the tube. Then he washed everything — the feeding tube site, the tube, and the syringe, and then he started washing all the dishes that were in the sink.

In the middle of doing the dishes, my mother started shrieking from the den. My father quickly dried his hands and ran to her. "What?" he asked her.

My mother just shrieked and pointed toward the doorway.

"Write it down," he said. "I don't know what you want."

She shrieked and pointed again. "Write it down," he said again.

She started crying, and my father returned to the kitchen, finished the dishes, and loaded up the dishwasher.

It hit me that my father did more than we realized, but my mother did not notice or appreciate it. My guess was that she was too caught up in the personal torment of her illness, and also frustrated that she could not easily express it. It seemed like her outbursts were the only way those painful and anguished feelings could come out and get vented.

And my mother was not the same person anymore. A sadness filled me as I realized that visiting them was no longer a happy, social occasion. It had become like visiting someone in a nursing home.

And I did not want to judge her. Who knew how well any of us would handle things if we were in the same condition?

Later that evening, we played a game of rummy tiles. By that time, my mother seemed to be feeling better, and she was laughing and enjoying the game. This time, she understood everything and made good combinations of the tiles, and she even won two of the games. That was a bit surprising and really good to see — she was relaxed and enjoying herself. I didn't see that very often anymore.

I went back to visit one week later. My mother showed me another machine, a small square box with a hose and mask coming out of it.

"What's that?"

She grabbed a piece of paper and wrote, "cough-assist."

"That's to help you cough?"

"It makes me cough to clear out the mucus in my throat so I won't choke so much."

"Does it help?"

"Yes, I feel better after using it."

"Mom, you're collecting all kinds of machines here. I hope you can keep straight which is which."

She laughed. "I promise I won't type on the cough-assist machine."

In early November my mother was about to turn 80. To help celebrate her birthday, my mother's two sisters, Fran and Ellen, and Ellen's husband Adam, flew out from New York to visit and stay for a week. In addition, my brother Stu and his wife Brenda flew down from Sacramento for a few days. It was going to be a big family celebration, and I was glad. This was a big birthday, and my mother really needed some fun and celebration in her life.

For this milestone birthday, I had previously asked family members from the East Coast to send me poems, letters, stories, and favorite memories of my mother. The pieces had been arriving for weeks in the mail. By the time we got together for the celebration, I had collected quite a few of them, and I knew my mother would love them. I planned to give them to her, along with all the gifts, right after dinner.

On the day of the party, the entire family, which came to nine of us, were going to meet at my parents' house in the afternoon.

Dustin and I got there a little earlier to see if my parents needed any help. When we got to the house, we saw that Fran was in the kitchen getting ready to feed my mom for lunch.

"Ruthie," Fran called out, holding a can of the liquid food in her hand. "Look, I have a nice birthday lunch for you," she said, and my mom grunted in response.

"First, this is your appetizer," Fran said, as she poured some of the nutrient-filled liquid into my mom's feeding tube. "See, this is shrimp cocktail. Isn't it good? And now I'm putting in French onion soup. Yum!"

A crooked smile touched my mother's lips. The tube was full, and Fran waited a minute until the liquid went down so that she could add in more.

As Fran poured in more of the liquid, she continued. "Now I'm putting in a nice big steak, just how you like it, medium rare. It's very tender and juicy." My mom laughed. "And now I'm putting in creamy garlic mashed potatoes with sour cream. And I'm also adding in green beans with almonds. Is it good?"

My mom laughed again, and it really warmed my heart to see them.

"Now it's time for dessert," Fran told my mom, as she got ready to pour in the last of the liquid. "First I'm putting in a big slice of strawberry shortcake." She waited a few seconds. Then she added, "And now I'm putting in chocolate ice cream. Do you like that?"

My mom nodded and barked out a laugh, her eyes on Fran. I could tell that she thoroughly enjoyed this. It was a great idea, and I wanted to remember to do this, if I would feed her later at some point.

After cleaning up, we then arranged extra chairs in the living room and got the house ready for the rest of the family. Within an hour, they started arriving.

The atmosphere was festive and joyful, and everyone was excitedly greeting each other, hugging, and talking. Happy shouts and laughter filled the air. We didn't get to see each other that often, and it felt really good to catch up with everyone.

We all sat down in the living room in a large circle of smiles and excited chatter. Everyone talked at once and over each other, back and forth across the circle. We were all so excited, no one could wait to speak, and it was a joyful free-for-all.

Before we all went out to dinner, my father fed my mother through the feeding tube in the kitchen, while the rest of the family continued chatting in the living room. When he finished feeding her, the group of nine of us drove in two cars to the restaurant where we had reservations.

The dinner was at a local Italian restaurant, and we could smell the delicious aromas as we approached the front doors. We were greeted by the hostess and were immediately shown to a back room that had been reserved for us. The room was filled with brightly colored balloons and there were festive mini-lights along the walls. Chairs surrounded one long table in the middle of the room, and we picked our seats, settling in rather noisily.

After looking at all the tantalizing choices on the menu, we ordered our meals. Hearing happy conversations about singing, dancing, movies, classes, dogs, and other topics, I felt myself brimming with an uncontained excitement. As we munched on the savory and satisfying food, with the delicious odors of garlic and tomato sauce filling our senses, the conversation settled down, and we eagerly dug into our food. My mother smiled throughout the entire meal, happy to be surrounded by her family, even if she could not join us in eating.

In honor of her birthday, my father had also hired a magician to come to the restaurant and do magic tricks for us, and it really helped to have that entire room to ourselves.

As we were finishing our dinners, the magician arrived, dressed in a bright red shirt and yellow vest. "Greetings everyone," he shouted, tipping his hat and smiling at each of us. "I am Markle the Magnificent, and I am here to entertain you with tricks you've never seen before." He then snapped his fingers, and a deck of cards appeared out of nowhere. He walked around the table, performing various tricks and close-up magic using multiple props inches away from our faces, and we were intrigued and baffled. His banter was funny, and he had all of us laughing, while we tried to figure out how he did everything.

As the magician was putting away the props from his last trick, the waiter came back into our room with a chocolate birthday cake topped with a lit candle. We all sang *Happy Birthday*, while my mom could not stop smiling.

After we finished the last of the birthday cake, we drove back to my parents' house and settled into the living room. There was a pile of festively wrapped presents in the corner, and my mother sat in the chair closest to them. When everyone was seated, we handed her the gifts one at a time, and she eagerly opened each package. Her face was radiant and she enjoyed every minute of it.

Once the gifts were all opened, I pushed aside the pile of discarded wrapping paper, and I then gave my mother all the notes, cards, poems, and stories that other family members had sent to me over the past couple months. That was an unexpected surprise for her and she clapped her hands happily. She glowed with joy while she looked at and read what everyone had sent, and we then read each one out loud to share with the rest of the family. It was uplifting to watch and I felt my heart soar.

At the end of the evening there were hugs all around and promises of getting together again soon. Fran was staying at their house for a few more days, and I was glad, as she would be able to give my mother a lot of love and support.

This birthday turned out even better than I had hoped. My mother had really needed it.

17

VARIOUS FRUSTRATIONS

My parents came to my house for a visit toward the end of November for my birthday. My mother seemed happy and upbeat. She brought along her Dynawrite machine, and I was glad to see that she was using it. We slowed down our conversation and waited for her to type in her words, so she could participate in our discussion.

"Mom," I asked her, "how are you with the new dosage of antidepressants? Are you feeling better?"

At first she shook her head no.

I asked her again, phrasing it differently. "Are you at least feeling more calm and relaxed about things? Less depressed, less anxious?"

This time she nodded and typed into the Dynawrite, and we heard the voice state, "I'm doing better."

"Good! Are you using the cough-assist machine?"

She laughed. "Sometimes."

"Have you had any more at-home help from the agency?"

She typed, "They have a four-hour minimum. That's too much. I want only one or two hours."

"Maybe you should put a notice on the bulletin board where you live asking for help. Maybe you can find someone that way for just one or two hours."

She typed, and we heard the machine's voice say, "Okay."

"Mom, please always know that we love you and want to help you. And always remember that you are not your body and not your illness. We love you."

She nodded. Not wanting to dwell only on her struggles with the disease, we then discussed happier topics, including my birthday plans for the weekend. We had a small birthday cake, and they left soon after that. It was a short visit, as she no longer had energy to stay for a long time.

We went to the next ALS support group meeting two weeks later, on a cool December day. The topics this time were relaxation, acceptance, and peace. There was no guest speaker at this meeting, so it went a little quicker. We listened to the others share various difficulties and what they had found that had helped them. We were still learning new things at these meetings, which was very rewarding.

My mother wrote a note, pushing it into my hand for me to share with the group. I told everyone that she found it hard to relax with this disease, and that it was difficult for her to find peace. Many others in the group responded with compassion and understanding, and the support we received really touched me. It made a huge difference in simply not feeling so alone.

When the meeting was over, my mother gave me a note saying that she's having trouble with her computer, that she couldn't read her e-mails. I said that I would look at it for her and try to see what the problem was.

I followed them back to their house and turned on her computer. It seemed that some of the settings had been changed and she could not find the icon she was used to seeing. I changed the settings for her and showed her how to do it herself. But I could tell that she was not following or understanding what I was saying. I showed her a few times, but she was simply not getting it. I asked her if she remembered how to reply to an e-mail, and she said no. I asked her if she knew how to close an e-mail. She just shrugged and said no.

A few minutes later, she cried and pointed at the screen. I asked her what was wrong. She wrote down "how do I move the arrow." I asked what arrow she meant, and she just pointed. Then I realized that she was referring to the cursor on the screen. I said, "Look, you move your mouse and the arrow moves." She just looked at me, confused.

I asked if she needed anything else, and she just pointed at the screen. I showed her where her e-mails were, and she started opening each one and reading them, one at a time. After a half-hour, seeing that all she wanted to do was catch up on her e-mails, I said good-bye and went home.

It bothered me that she seemed to be losing cognitive ability and comprehension where the computer was concerned. Those were skills that she once knew and had mastered. I realized that the computer was becoming too difficult for her to use, and that she would not be using it for much longer.

I visited my parents twice in January. Both times, my mother was crying and shrieking. During those visits, I tried numerous times to talk to her, communicate with her, reach for her hand, and show her love and compassion. But she pulled back from me and didn't appear to want any contact with me. It seemed that she was too immersed in her own anguish, and there was no connection and no communication. If she was not crying, she was staring and unresponsive. I did not stay long on those days. It tore me up inside, but I simply did not know how to reach her or help her.

My brother called me toward the end of January. "I spoke to Mom's doctor about her antidepressants," he said. "The doctor is changing her prescription to a different antidepressant again because of the side effects, so he is now prescribing a new one. But this is good, it's a serotonin uptake inhibitor, which is what we want. Mom is being switched over gradually, and hopefully this will be good for her."

"Good," I told him, "She needs something, she's been really miserable lately. I really appreciate you helping with this."

After hanging up, I thought about my mother's condition, and all the help we tried to give her. She was still keeping me at a distance and I felt shut out, but there was not much I could do about it. I wanted her to choose what was comfortable for her, no matter how it made me feel. If she wanted to keep me at a distance and not let me get too close, I would respect that. But I at least wanted to make sure she knew that I loved her.

In February, Dustin and I went to visit my parents for my father's birthday. It was cool and cloudy, and I didn't need my sunglasses, which did not happen very often. Traffic was slow, and the drive seemed to take forever, which gave me more time to worry about my mother and think about the BiPAP machine, the cough-assist machine, the feeding tube, all the times she had fallen, and now deterioration of her mental faculties.

As I parked the car in front of their house, I hoped my mother was having a good day. I never knew what to expect anymore when we visited.

We rang the bell and they both answered the door. My mother was smiling this time, and I felt myself sigh with relief.

We sat down in the den, with my parents taking their favorite spots on the couch. My mother was alert and rational, and she seemed to comprehend everything. She even made the effort to participate in our conversation, sometimes handing us notes, and sometimes using the Dynawrite machine.

The day was relaxed and easy, as we talked and shared stories. My dad opened his presents like a happy kid. One of his gifts was his favorite soup from our local deli. This was something special for him, since he did not get home-cooked meals anymore, and he was thrilled.

My mom laughed and joined in, and she actually seemed more like her old self. I asked her if she was feeling better on the new medication, and she shook her head no.

"Is there any change at all?"

She wrote, "No, I feel the same." Then she added, "I still cry a lot."

"Mom, crying is also a symptom of the disease," I said, and she nodded. "You don't seem sad or depressed today."

She handed me another note. "I laugh a lot, too."

I smiled at her. "That's nice. That is also part of the disease. Enjoy *that* part."

She smiled back at me.

"Are you having any other problems?" She shook her head no. I glanced at her arm, but I did not see any spasms.

We went for a short walk in the afternoon. It was a little warmer by then, with a light, fresh breeze, which was perfect for being outside. We probably walked only about a half-mile, but my mother walked so slowly that it took us close to an hour. She used her new walker, which kept her more stable. It felt like we were a normal family, walking outside together in the fresh air and getting a little exercise, even if it took a long time.

Dustin and I had brought food with us, so we prepared dinner, without my parents having to do anything. My father first fed my mother through the feeding tube, and then we set the table. After we ate the salad and salmon, we placed a custard pie on the table and put a candle in it. We sang *Happy Birthday* to my dad, and he grinned happily throughout the off-key rendition of the song. My mother did not have any of the food that we had served — until we got to the ice cream. Then she perked up and looked at us happily, and she ate a bowl of chocolate ice cream. I was glad that she could still eat and enjoy that, even if some of it ended up on her face and her bib.

A few minutes after eating the ice cream, my mother choked a few times, as though her lungs were not strong enough to clear the mucus from her throat. We were alarmed, but she then settled down and she was okay after that.

After clearing the dishes, we played rummy tiles for a few hours, and my mother did better than I expected. She did not seem confused, and it felt like old times, happy and carefree, almost like a reprieve from her illness.

I also noticed, to my surprise, that my father was warm and loving and helpful, and he was attentive to my mother's needs. I hoped that he was becoming more accepting of her condition and more willing to help her.

At the end of the evening, when we were leaving, my father hugged me and said very lovingly, "Oh, I've missed you." His words touched me deeply. But I didn't think he realized that it was he, not I, who had changed so much.

And I wondered whether that was one of the reasons my mother seemed happier today and was functioning at a higher level. I felt like we were all moving in a positive direction.

Driving home, I thought about how nice it was to see my mother laughing and feeling good again. Maybe everything was interrelated and each part of the puzzle helped another part, making all of it work smoother and easier. I didn't want to think about it too long and jinx it, so I put on the car radio and happily sang along to "Daydream Believer" by The Monkees.

18

PERSPECTIVES, PODIATRY, AND DISTRESS

Over the next couple of weeks, I received phone calls from Stu, Fran, and Ellen. They each were concerned about my mother and worried that enough wasn't being done to help her in every way possible. We discussed her need for privacy, her waning independence, her need for help, my father's willingness and limitations with helping her, and what has been done up until now. After much discussion, we agreed that there were no easy answers.

Everyone had a different opinion, and I knew that love for my mother and frustration at the situation played with everyone's emotions.

I started thinking that we *all* were right. Each of us held one piece of the truth, and each of our opinions was valid, but none of us had the entire truth. None of us saw everything or really knew how my mother felt. My mother showed a different side to each of us, and she responded to each of us differently. She opened up to us and shared with each of us in varying ways, and she answered questions differently to each of us. And we each also reached her and saw her on different days, and her situation varied each time

— different moods, feelings, and levels of independence. And on top of that, we each had a different perspective to begin with, and we tended to see through our own filters and expectations. So there was no one right answer. And each of our truths did not negate another's truth, they were all valid and could co-exist.

And maybe all the different perspectives together approached the *real* truth, whatever that was. But even that, I knew, kept changing.

I shared all these thoughts with my family, although I knew everyone was trying to find the elusive correct answer and insist on their opinion. I hoped that helped my family to understand, but I wasn't sure.

Later that month, the four of us went to the next ALS support group meeting. The guest speaker was a nurse from Gresham Falls Community Hospital who specialized in helping ALS patients. Her main focus at this meeting was to talk about some of the experimental clinical drug trials that were going on to help ALS patients. Going into detail about each drug, she told us that some of them were promising and some were not.

I asked her if my mother would be eligible for any of these clinical trials since she is technically diagnosed with PLS and not ALS, and the nurse said that she did not know if she would be eligible for these trials, but that any doctor could still prescribe the drugs for her and see what happens. She said that any drugs that already have FDA approval or are beyond a certain phase of testing can simply be prescribed. For drugs that have not, the doctor can petition the FDA for approval for their use as orphan drugs or for compassionate use, and the doctor can then try them. So this would really be up to her doctor, if he was willing to do this.

The nurse also discussed the BiPAP machine that my mother was using. She said that patients must use it a minimum of four hours per day to get real benefit from it.

I asked my mother how much she used it. She wrote that she uses it one hour per day. I told her to try for two hours, and she nodded and laughed. I suggested that she use it when she watched TV so she would be distracted and not notice it as much, and she said that's what she did.

The nurse also talked about feeding tubes, and my mother wanted me to contribute her experience to the group. So I shared with everyone that my mother now had a feeding tube, that she was happy with it, and I told them what kind of food she was putting in the tube. Some members in the group said they were glad for her, and others shared their experiences, all positive, with a feeding tube. It seemed that everyone who had a feeding tube was pleased with it and glad they had it. They all said that they were feeling better since they were using it.

It was another good meeting, and we hugged the others in the group as we left.

As we were walking to our cars, my mother handed me a note saying that she would like to get a shower chair with a back so she can sit on it when she takes a shower. I told her that she can get one in any medical supply store, like where she got the support bars that go around her toilet, and she said okay.

She then handed me another note. "Dad doesn't help me."

I looked at her face, and I could see the anguish. "Mom, I have seen him go out of his way to help you and try to please you. He really does a lot. Please don't expect perfection. He is only human, he is doing what he can, and he is really working hard to please you. Even trained nurses won't meet every need every time." She nodded at this, and I continued. "Don't expect to have *all* your needs met *all* the time, just most of the time, okay? Nothing is perfect in this world. And Dad is really trying. He loves you and cares about you and is doing his best. Try to see that and let him know you appreciate what he is doing for you."

She looked at me and nodded, and I hoped this made sense to her. I thought she had unreasonable expectations, maybe because she was feeling more needy, but she seemed to understand and accept what I said. I thought that maybe now she might be able to recognize my father's efforts a little more.

We hugged and I watched them drive away. I hoped I was helping and was making a difference for her.

"Your mother has a corn on one toe and it is painful," my father told me when he called in early April.

"Has she seen a doctor?"

"Yes, and her doctor recommended surgery."

"I know a good podiatrist near me who I've been to. Before she has surgery, have her come to my podiatrist and get a second opinion. Maybe she doesn't need the surgery."

"Okay, I'll tell her."

"Good. And how are you doing? Are you okay?"

"Yes, but I have a lot of pain in my left leg."

"Why? What happened?"

"I don't know what's wrong. I have not seen a doctor yet."

"Are you walking okay?"

"I'm using your mother's walker."

"But she needs that."

"She hangs on to the side of it when we walk."

"Go to the doctor and get it checked out," I told him. "And make sure Mom is stable with the walker when she's on the side of it."

A week later, on a cool and cloudy morning, my parents came to my house so I could take them to the appointment with my podiatrist.

My father said he had seen a doctor and his leg was feeling better. It turned out that he had strained a hamstring, and it was healing. Neither of my parents was using the walker that day. They both just hobbled along slowly, holding onto each other.

I drove my parents the short distance to the medical building to see the podiatrist. After a short wait, we were all shown into a small treatment room.

"Hi, I'm Dr. Larson," a good-looking middle-aged man said smiling, as he came into the treatment room. "What seems to be the problem?" He had a very nice, gentle bedside manner, and he spoke warmly to my mother and made her feel at ease.

After we explained the problem, Dr. Larson examined her foot, and then he cut back the corn and gave her a pad that was cut to fit her toe so it would be more comfortable. He said that she did not need surgery at this time, that she could just come in periodically if needed, and he would cut back the corn and give her new pads. And he said that if she ever wanted, she could have the surgery done any time. He described it as minor outpatient surgery with just local anesthesia. Then he cut all her toenails and rubbed cream into her feet. I loved how kind and good he was with her. My mother walked out happy, without any pain.

We then went back to my house for lunch. First my mother was fed with the feeding tube, and then the rest of us heartily stuffed ourselves with bagels, lox, and cream cheese. After we ate, I brought out some ice cream, and my mother's eyes lit up. We had two flavors — chocolate and vanilla with caramel swirl in it. My mom pointed to both, her eyes big and happy. We filled up a bowl for her and she smiled the whole time she ate.

My father was in a supportive mood and seemed to be enjoying his role as a helper. Whenever my mother pointed to him, he would smile and guess what she needed, almost like a game, and he was usually right. Sometimes it was a tissue, sometimes a pen, and sometimes something else. When he guessed right, my mother nodded, and my father supplied whatever it was to her. This time, it was a tissue, and my father got it on the first guess.

My mother gave a garbled laugh and handed me a note. "Dad is a really cute tissue dispenser."

Toward the end of April we went to another ALS support group meeting. A guest speaker addressed the topic of hospice, informing us about what it was, how it could help, and how to go about obtaining it. However, every time the speaker used the word "terminal," my mother started crying, and each time it happened, her crying got louder. I softly stroked her arm, but she did not stop crying.

The speaker stopped and gazed at my mother several times, but my mother continued to cry. After this happened a few times, the speaker finally stopped talking and looked compassionately at my mother.

"I understand this is upsetting to you," she said quietly, "but your crying is a bit disruptive to the group. I'm sorry, but I need to ask you to please go outside until you calm down so we can continue the meeting. When you calm down, you are welcome to come back." She smiled kindly at my mother, but my mother turned red, and I felt embarrassed for her.

The three of us promptly gathered our belongings and went outside. We sat on a bench under a tree while my mother continued to cry. After about 15 minutes, my mother said she wanted to go home.

"Are you sure?" I asked her.

She nodded and stood up, and I watched them walk to their car and drive away. I glanced back at the meeting, sorry that we were missing it. Then I got in my car and drove home as well, thoughts swirling around in my head. I guessed that she still had at least a few years left, but no matter how much time she had remaining, I thought that hospice services would be good for her. And I also understood that all of these issues could be difficult and overwhelming to face. I figured that she would accept those services when she was ready, and my job was to be loving and compassionate, rather than forcing the issues.

19

LAUNDRY, FALLING, AND LAS VEGAS

Stu came down for another visit in the beginning of May. He said that our mom had told him that she wanted to be in an assisted living facility. I drove over there and joined my brother and my parents.

We asked my mother if she really wanted to be in an assisted living facility. She nodded yes, and we asked her why. She wrote down, "So I can eat better meals."

"Mom, you can't eat regular meals, you have a feeding tube."

She looked at me blankly.

"Mom, you don't need assisted living for that. And you don't really want to leave your home, do you?"

She said nothing.

"She does not need an assisted living facility," my father said. "She should stay here at home."

"Mom, I'm not even sure an assisted living facility would help you with feedings through your feeding tube. That may be beyond the scope of what they would normally do." My mother had no response. "Mom, I don't think you would be happy there. I think you would feel even worse. You would be happiest in your own home."

She shrugged and looked down at the floor.

A week later, on a warm day with puffy clouds dotting the sky, Dustin and I visited my parents for Mother's Day. We gave my mom a wrapped gift, and she happily tore off the paper and opened the box. She smiled, held up the pink blouse, and nodded at us.

My mom typed into the Dynawrite machine and the machine's female voice said, "thank you." We spent an easy afternoon talking and even my mom joined in.

In the evening, she handed me a note. "This was a nice day. I'm feeling good today, and I'm glad you are here."

I went back to see my parents in June. My mother was smiling and seemed happy, and we talked easily. We kept the pace of the conversation slow, and she wrote down notes and joined in the conversation.

When it was time to eat, my father fed her through the feeding tube, and then the rest of us sat down to eat. As we were happily eating and talking about how good the food was, my mother went into the den and started crying. It hit me that it was too painful for her to watch us eat. I realized that meals were a strong and powerful reminder of how much she was missing, of how much she could not do anymore. It was another sign of how sick she was, of how broken down her body was. Dustin went into the den and turned on the TV to distract her, but we could still hear her crying, and my heart felt heavy.

After dinner, we joined her in the den and she stopped crying. But throughout the conversation, she was drooling and wiping at her chin with a tissue. I could see that the reminders were really always there. She could not get away from them.

I told them how Dustin was building a deck in our backyard around our above-ground pool, and what a great job he was doing. "I'm so proud of him — it is coming out great," I said. "It looks so luxurious and professional. Well, except where he fucked up." My mother laughed. Her laugh sounded like a strange, strangled noise. I didn't care what it sounded like, I just kept trying to talk about similar things that would make her laugh again.

I thanked my father for all that he was doing, and I let him know that we saw how much he did and that we appreciated it. He smiled at me and gave me a big hug. I didn't think he heard that enough, and he really needed to hear it more.

We went to another ALS support group meeting in July. When we shared our stories, I told the group how my mother was doing with the feeding tube. The leader asked my mom to show thumbs up or thumbs down whether she was glad she got the feeding tube. She immediately showed thumbs up. Then I told the group how she hated cooking so she was now freed from that chore and never had to do that again, and my mother started laughing. Hearing the strange sound, the leader looked concerned at first, until she understood that my mother was laughing. I realized that this group rarely saw her laugh.

My father then shared the fact that he had now learned where all the stores are. As they drive, he said, Ruth wouldn't speak, but she would point to turn here or turn there. He said that she points, points, points with her finger, and he demonstrated, jabbing his index finger around the room.

My mother scribbled a quick note that I shared with the group. "She says that's how she gives him the finger," I told them, and everyone laughed.

My mother then wrote another note and asked the group about lithium and whether anyone there had experience with it. Someone had recommended the medicine to her for her mood swings, but her doctor advised against it, so she wanted to know what others thought. The leader said that she heard that it doesn't really help and there had been reports of bad side effects, too. She suggested that my mother talk to and listen to her own doctor.

In August, I received an e-mail from my mother. She wrote that she fell in the garage and hurt her shoulder. I immediately called my father.

"Dad, what happened to Mom?"

"She fell. She went to the hospital and she had x-rays taken, but we don't know the results yet."

"I'm so sorry. How is she feeling?"

"She's depressed."

"Please tell her I love her and am thinking of her and hope she feels better."

After I got off the phone, I sent my mother a get-well card.

Then I heard from Stu, Fran, and Ellen. They all were concerned and wanted to help, but there was nothing to do. Underneath it all, I think all of us just wanted her to be healthy. And that was something that we could not fix, no matter what we did.

My father called back a few days later. "The x-rays showed that she has arthritis in her shoulder, but it's minor."

"Was anything broken or fractured?"

"No, nothing was broken, and she is feeling better. However, they said that she is anemic."

"Anemic?"

"And they also said that she has kidney problems."

"What? Kidney problems? What does that mean?"

"I don't know, they didn't tell me any other details. That's all they told me."

I called my brother and asked him if he knew anything.

"Yes," Stu said, after I asked him about this. "I spoke to Mom's doctor. He told me that she is slightly anemic, but she's okay and not to worry. He then said that other than having ALS, she's actually in good health."

His words struck me as both sad and funny, and an awkward laugh came out of me.

I then received an e-mail from my mother. She wrote, "The x-rays showed an arthritic condition of my scapula and tendinitis of my right shoulder. I feel better. It doesn't hurt anymore. I'm off the pain pills. As for the anemia, I'm only off by one point, so they mark it low. Same for the kidneys, I'm only off one point there too, so they mark it low. But I'm fine."

That made sense to me, but I hoped she was really okay and that this was not the start of any additional medical problems.

In September, my father called me. "We're going to Las Vegas for a few days," he said.

"Are you sure that's a good idea? Is Mom up for that? That might be hard for her."

"She's fine and she's looking forward to it," he said. "I'm bringing her food and will feed her through the feeding tube. She'll be okay."

Las Vegas was about a six-hour drive from where they lived, and they easily made the trek. I worried about my mother the whole time they were there, and I hoped that there would not be any trouble.

As soon as they got back, I called and spoke to my father. He had no problems to report — he had fed my mother in their hotel room through the feeding tube, and then he went out to eat at a restaurant by himself. They had a great time at one of the shows, where they saw an Elvis impersonator. I felt really good hearing that she could still get around and do some things that were fun.

I worried about her a lot and wanted to keep her safe, but I also knew that she truly needed more fun and joy in her life, and this was good for her.

20

More Confusion and Another Fall

My parents came to our house at the end of the month for a visit. My mother said she was all healed from her fall and she was feeling good. They told me all about their trip to Las Vegas, going into detail about the hotel, the food, the gambling, the shows, and everything they did.

We then went in our backyard and I showed them the deck Dustin was building. My mother walked slowly and stepped carefully. I worried about her with the few steps up to the deck, but she got around okay and seemed stable.

About an hour later, my mother started choking, as though she had too much phlegm in the back of her throat and couldn't clear it. It sounded like mucus was blocking her from breathing properly. She kept choking until she was out of breath. The choking probably lasted less than a minute, but it seemed like so much longer. After she stopped choking, her breathing was labored and she had a hard time catching her breath.

"Mom," I said, once she was breathing more normally, "are you choking more now?"

She nodded yes.

"Are you using your cough-assist and BiPAP breathing machines?"

A strangled laugh came out of her.

"You're supposed to use the BiPAP three or four hours a day, right?"

She handed me a note. "I use it maybe once a week."

"Maybe you should use it more than that. It would help keep your lungs stronger and healthier longer. And what about the cough-assist machine, are you using that?"

She laughed again, that same strangled sound.

I figured that those machines must be uncomfortable to use. And as much as we all knew these devices could help her — and she no doubt knew that more than any of us — it really was her choice whether or not to use them.

When it was time for dinner, we decided to go to a local deli. My mother handed me a note saying that she would not join us, that she wanted to just stay in our house while we went out.

"Are you sure? That's what you want? You'll be okay?" She nodded yes.

My father fed her with the feeding tube, and then we set up the TV for my mother to watch while we were gone. After she was settled in, my father, Dustin, and I went out to eat. We promised her that we wouldn't be gone long.

As we were munching on our deli sandwiches and pickles, I realized that it was too painful for her to watch other people eat, knowing that she could no longer eat the way others could. It had to be extremely frustrating, especially when sitting at a table in a restaurant. I could certainly understand why she would rather stay home and not join us.

We ate quickly and rushed back to the house. And after we got back home, we all were talking and laughing, including my mother. When our sweet little dog Peanut, wagging her tail, timidly approached my father, he tried to shoo her away. So I explained to Peanut that good people are kind to dogs and that my father is a freak. My mother loved that and started laughing.

A few minutes later, she wrote some things on the Dynawrite machine that made no sense: "drool protective what thing is my machine." We all read what she wrote, but none of us understood the message she was showing us. She looked at it and showed it to each of us again, but we still didn't understand it. She looked frustrated, and then she started crying. I ached for her, and I wished I could know what she was trying to say.

Later that night, we guessed that maybe she was trying to tell us that she needed her cough-assist machine that cleans out her excess mucus, but that she had left it at home. It disturbed me to think how unclear the communication was becoming at times.

I found that I felt compassionate toward my father, and my heart went out to him, since he had to deal with this every day. It was getting harder to understand her messages. I knew that *both* my parents needed a lot of compassion and love.

Not long after that, I realized that I now rarely received e-mails from my mother. I thought that it must be getting harder for her. It seemed like she was starting to forget how to use the computer and she got frustrated. She no longer knew how to respond to an e-mail and she got online only once or twice a week to read her e-mails.

In January when I visited my parents, my mom looked serious.

"Hi Mom, how are you feeling?" I asked her, concern creeping into my voice.

She handed me a note that said "I'm getting worse."

"How? What is happening?"

She wrote, "I'm now on a feeding tube."

"Mom, you've had that for a year now. Is everything else okay?"

She handed me another note. "My doctor said I now have ALS."

"Not PLS? It's now ALS?"

She nodded and a tear rolled down her cheek.

"I'm sorry, Mom." I reached for her hand. I did not want to even think about the implications of that.

Then she suddenly pointed to the computer and gave me a note saying, "Not working."

Dustin looked at her computer. It seemed that someone who had children had recently visited them, and they had loaded a few games onto her computer for their kids to play, and they also had changed the configuration of the main screen, so my mother didn't know what to do. Dustin spent an hour deleting and uninstalling the kids' games. He finally got the computer to work normally, the way it used to, and we firmly told both my parents not to let anyone else touch their computer.

While he was still working on the computer, I tried talking more to my mother. However, she now seemed more distant, and whatever I said or asked, she ignored me and cried on and off. When I asked her questions, for the most part I got no response. Sometimes she nodded yes, sometimes she shook her head no, and sometimes both. But most of the time, she just stared and did not respond.

Dustin was finishing up on the computer and testing it out, and I went back to watching him work to see how it was going. Suddenly, we heard a loud crash and a thud, and we turned around to see what had fallen — it was my mother. She was on the floor in the doorway coming from the kitchen into the den, her legs splayed out at a strange angle. She looked dazed and startled, and then she started to cry.

We immediately jumped up and ran to her. "Mom, are you okay? Are you hurt?" I asked.

She just stared at me, and then she resumed softly weeping. We struggled to get her up off the floor, and we eased her into a chair. She stopped crying, took a deep breath, and looked at us.

"Are you okay?"

She did not respond, but she did not seem to be in pain.

Then she picked up her pant legs and showed me a big bump and an older bruise on her shin and another bruise around her ankle.

"What happened? Did you fall earlier?"

"She fell a few weeks ago," my father replied.

"Mom, please use the walker in the house to stay safe, okay?"

She just stared back at me, without any further response.

I also noticed that there was a somewhat sour smell around her. I couldn't tell if it was coming from her clothes or her skin. But being that I was not getting much response from her and the communication was so poor, I decided not to say anything right then. I figured that I would follow up with that another time when she was feeling better.

A few minutes later, we heard her coughing and choking. The sounds were feeble, like her lungs were weak. It seemed that she was not able to cough very well on her own.

We also realized that she was getting stiffer. Her muscles and limbs seemed rigid. When we tried to help her stand up from the couch, it seemed that it was harder to pull her up because she was so inflexible and awkward, and she was unable to help us.

We asked my father if he noticed that she was confused.

"No," he said emphatically. "She still plays a good game of bridge a few times a week."

That seemed incongruent with what we were seeing and I doubted that it was true. However, I did not want to force the issue and risk a fight.

I hoped that this was just a bad day and maybe she still had many good days.

After we got home, I sent an e-mail to my family to update them on her status. I reminded them that this was a progressive illness and that she would continue to get worse, but that she was seeing her doctor regularly and was being monitored.

"Let's not turn ourselves inside out trying to find the perfect solution," I wrote to the family. "From what I can see, the best we can do is let her know that we love her and care about her. Let's also encourage her to enjoy whatever she can still do, and focus on that. Even just sitting in the backyard and breathing the fresh air — there is always something that can bring her joy, and she needs to find and do those."

I then spoke to Julie, the ALS caseworker, with my concerns about my mother falling more often and her poor communication.

"Yes, your observations are very much in line with mine," she said. "It is very difficult to understand what Ruth wants, and her communication is not good. It is hard to know how much she understands when you talk to her."

"She is not clear on the Dynawrite, either."

"No, she's not. I think that is getting to be too hard for her. The typing is difficult, and Ruth has too many misspelled words and rambling thoughts, so it's hard to figure out."

"I don't like that she is still falling. I wish she'd use the walker, even in the house."

"I agree. I also suggested to both of them that Ruth use the walker in the house, but Eric said no, and he insisted that there was no reason for her to use it inside."

"I'm afraid she will fall again."

"Yes, me too. And I also strongly urged them to get a lightweight wheelchair for Ruth to use when she's out shopping or running errands. I'm very concerned that one day her legs will fail her and she will take a serious fall, possibly hitting her head on concrete, and possibly sustaining a traumatic brain injury or an aneurysm. Or she may break a hip. She really needs the stability and safety of a wheelchair."

"I wish we could insist on that."

"Well, Eric told me absolutely not, he will not allow it. I don't know why he is so resistant to her using a wheelchair. It's for safety reasons. It would even be easier for him to push her in a wheelchair than to have her hold onto his arm when she walks. I wish her doctor would insist that she get a wheelchair. Maybe you could talk to her doctor about that."

"Okay, I will."

"Ruth showed me the laundry room where their clothes were piled on the floor. Apparently their washer or dryer stopped working and they are waiting to get it fixed."

"So they can't do any laundry at all now?"

"No. And I am not sure why Ruth wanted to show me this other than she may have wanted me to find out that Eric still expects her to do the laundry and he is leaving it for her. Eric again said this is the only thing he does not do and will not do, that it's Ruth's job. He even said that the exercise is good for her."

"That's horrible! And I thought he was now helping with that."

"Lynn, I think Ruth's condition is deteriorating and that she is probably very fatigued all the time. She may not feel up to doing any kind of housework or laundry at all."

"Yes, that would make sense. I will talk to him."

Her next sentence gripped me and made the hairs on my neck stand up. "In my opinion, Lynn, I think Ruth is very close to being appropriate for enrolling in hospice. But most likely, Ruth and Eric will not want to consider it."

"I know hospice is scary and upsetting for her."

"Yes. And although Ruth will probably think and be fearful that it is a death sentence to have hospice care, there are other ALS patients who have been under hospice care for well over a year, and some even longer. If Ruth had a hospice team coming in to see her, she would see a nurse once a week, and she would have a nursing assistant come to bathe her two or three times a week. She would have other therapy services if needed, therapy visits, and she would have whatever medical equipment and prescription drugs she needs. Medicare hospice pays for everything, so it wouldn't cost them anything."

"I will talk to them. But I know my mother sees hospice as a death sentence, and she will be very resistant to it. I also know that my father thinks that he is handling everything fine and they don't need help. So the thought of hospice, her deteriorating condition, and death, are issues that could easily be beyond their coping abilities right now."

"I understand that, Lynn. Good luck when you talk to them."

After hanging up, I thought about what we said, and I knew this would be a very tough conversation to have with them.

21

Hospice Information

Stu was able to get the names of the people my parents played bridge with, and he called them. He asked each one if our mother still played bridge reasonably well. One of them said they refused to play bridge with her but they didn't want to say anything more than that. Another said, "Ruth really isn't as sharp as she used to be." Another said, "Well, Ruth still *tries* to play, and that's all I'll say." So although my father kept insisting that she still played bridge, as though that was a badge of proof that she was okay, her cognitive abilities had obviously deteriorated. She was not the same person she used to be. This was another reminder not to trust my father's judgment of her condition.

I didn't know whether or not my mother even still liked or wanted to play bridge, but I decided not to ask her. I spoke to my brother about this and expressed my concerns.

"I agree with you," Stu said. "She is definitely not playing bridge the way she used to, and she definitely gets confused."

"So we really can't take Dad's word for anything."

"No, we can't. Dad keeps insisting that everything is okay, but it's not." He cleared his throat and then continued. "I'm going to call her doctor and tell him to recommend that she get a wheelchair. I think she really needs one."

"I agree. And when you speak to the doctor, also ask him to recommend hospice care. I really think it's time for that, too."

I then spoke to Julie. She told me that most hospice care is provided to terminally ill patients in their own homes by a Medicare-certified hospice nursing agency. In order to enroll in hospice, the patient's primary physician must say he thinks his patient may only live six months or less. However, many hospice patients live beyond that time and, at six months, they just need to go back to their doctor and get another order for hospice services so that it will continue.

Julie's next words gripped me. "I really feel that Ruth is deteriorating very quickly, especially since she is not using the BiPAP or cough-assist machine. In fact, I am surprised that she has not already landed in the hospital with aspiration pneumonia or a respiratory infection. If her vital lung capacity happens to be less than 30 percent, her prognosis is not good. Her doctor would have no problem in ordering hospice care for Ruth. The bigger problem will be getting her to accept their services. Every physician should talk with their patients who have serious medical conditions about what their end-of-life options are, including hospice, and I hope he talks to her about this."

"What exactly would hospice do for her?"

"I will send you information. Basically, hospice helps the patient be as comfortable as possible so that they can have the best quality of life for whatever time they have left. The focus is on caring for the patient, not curing any disease."

"Keeping her comfortable would be good."

"I also recommend that Ruth fill out advance health-care directives, if she has not already done so."

"Yes, I agree, that is important. I will make sure she does that."

One day later, I received the information about hospice programs, and it filled me with a heavy sadness.

I shared the information with Stu, Fran, and Ellen. Immediately, I received many responses saying that we should insist that my mother use the breathing and cough-assist machines every day.

I called and responded to each family member, explaining that we had brought this up to her many times. "Ruth knows she is supposed to use them, but she doesn't like to," I told everyone.

"But it will keep her healthier and prolong her life," everyone vehemently insisted.

"It's her choice," I patiently explained, as I had many times before, "and it cannot be forced on her. We need to honor her choices regarding all assistive devices, and respect whatever she chooses, whether or not we agree with it. It's *her* choice, not ours."

I then sent an e-mail to everyone explaining in detail that it is the patient's choice for all of these optional devices, whether it was for breathing machines, feeding tubes, or even ventilators. My mother chose to go on a feeding tube, but not all patients choose that. Some patients feel that a ventilator gives them much more life, more energy, and more time, and they wholeheartedly use it. Other patients choose not to use them, and would rather not be tied down to a machine that they feel is uncomfortable or difficult, even if they pass away sooner. They may choose to not prolong a painful and difficult living situation. That is their choice and should *always* be their choice. As much as we want to help and prolong someone's life, no one is really in a position to make those decisions for anyone else. I told them that our role is to support her no matter what and respect and honor all her decisions and choices.

Ellen then called me. "Lynn, I'm glad you said that, and I agree with you. The day my best friend died, I was in her house with her. She had been sick for a long time, and she was not well that day. She seemed to be having trouble breathing. So I called her doctor and told him to come over right away. My friend got very upset and made me call him back and cancel the appointment, which I did. She died that night. I think that was what she chose to do. So I agree with you. You can't force someone. Ruthie is still rational and entitled to make her own decisions. We could make suggestions, but that's it. It's really up to her."

In early February, Dustin and I went to my parents' house for my father's birthday. My father fed my mother through the feeding tube, and then the rest of us dug into the bowls of tuna salad, egg salad, green salad, and rolls. This time my mother stayed with us in the kitchen while we ate lunch, and she seemed okay. Then we put a candle in a little cake we had brought, and we sang *Happy Birthday* to my father.

We had brought along our dog, Peanut, and my mother smiled at the dog and tried to play with her. My mother giggled like a happy little girl, holding onto a stuffed, floppy elephant and playing tug-of-war with Peanut.

I was glad to see that my mom was walking around the house with her walker, but I saw that she needed help getting up and down from the couch in the den. Once she was up, she was independent and used the walker to move around. But I wondered how she got up from the couch if no one was there to help her.

I tried to go out of my way to talk to my mother, even though communication was difficult. I wanted to include her and make sure she felt loved and valued. But to all my questions, even simple yes-or-no questions, there was barely a response. Most of the time my questions were met with just a stare. A few times, she tried writing down a response, but her answers were confusing. She wrote down one sentence three times, the same words, but they made no sense.

My mother then pointed to the computer. "Do you want me to turn on the computer?" I asked her. She nodded yes.

I turned on the computer and navigated to her e-mails. Once there, I noticed that she had e-mails from over a month earlier that had not yet been read.

"Mom, are you reading your e-mails?" First she nodded yes, then she shook her head no.

"Is it too hard for you to work the computer?"

She handed me a note. "Take it away, it is a pain in the ass."

"Are you sure? You don't want it anymore?"

She handed me another note. "Yes, take it away, I don't like it, it's too hard."

"No," my father blurted out. "We'll keep it. I'll use it."

I looked back and forth at each of my parents. "Okay," I finally said, "Dad, I'll teach you how to use it." But I knew that would be difficult. He was not very good with technology, and he even had trouble setting his watch or using the microwave. So I had my doubts, but I thought I would at least let him try.

My mother then started coughing, but the cough was weak. Fortunately, it lasted only one or two minutes. She then looked for a tissue, but unable to find one, she started crying. Realizing what she wanted, I jumped up and brought her a box of tissues, and she stopped crying right away. It seemed that her frustration and tolerance levels were low. That was understandable, and it hurt to think about what daily life was like for her.

At the end of the day, when we hugged good-bye, I noticed that she again smelled very stale and slightly sickly. I wondered if maybe it was the drool that drips and gets on everything. I did not say anything, as I thought they were doing the best they could, and I did not want to make her more uncomfortable.

The following weekend, I went back to show my father how to use the computer. As we sat down at the machine, I saw that my mother had put large stickers that said "chocolate" all over the computer keyboard. As I removed all the stickers and explained to my dad that those were not a necessary part of the computer's operating system and would not help him type better, my mother laughed.

I then patiently explained everything multiple times, and I gave him a printed cheat sheet that he could refer to. I had him log on and check e-mails himself a few times to make sure he could do it by himself. To my surprise, he actually did better than I had expected.

Then we took a break from the computer and turned our attention to my mom. "So how are you doing? Is everything okay? Any problems?"

She smiled and handed me a note. "Dad is finally doing the laundry."

"Really? Dad, you're helping Mom with the laundry now? Is the machine fixed?"

My father made a face showing that he had finally given in. "Yeah, I realized she needed help with that. I'm now doing the laundry. And the machine is fine; I wasn't pushing the right buttons before, but now I know what to do, so there's no problem."

I wondered briefly whether he had deliberately not been working the machine correctly to avoid doing it, but I decided to not address that. "Yay, Dad — that's great! Thank you for doing that, I know Mom really does need help with that."

"Well, I'm doing just about everything now."

"Good," I told him. "It's a lot easier for you to do things than it is for her." I paused and then added, "And please know that we really appreciate you doing so much."

My father smiled, and he seemed much more relaxed than he had been for months. I hoped that meant that he would keep helping her even more.

It also meant that hospice care could be put off a little while longer. I felt reluctant to bring up that topic, and I hoped that if all my mother's needs were being taken care of and she did not have to do any housework, life for her would be easier and less stressful, and maybe she wouldn't need hospice services for a while yet. With my father doing the laundry, things seemed to be going better now, and I hoped that I was being realistic. I did not want to even think that maybe I was now the one in denial.

22

A Fractured Hip

"Your mother fell again," my father told me on the phone one week later. "She's in the hospital."

"What happened?"

"She was in the kitchen this past weekend and she fell. She was in a lot of pain, so I took her to the hospital. They took x-rays and found that she had fractured her left hip. She had surgery this morning and she's now in recovery."

"Oh my God, is she okay? Did the surgery go well?"

"She's fine, I was with her the whole time."

He gave me the phone number for the hospital, and I called up and spoke to the nurse. The nurse told me that my mother had arthroplasty, which is the reconstruction of a damaged joint. When I asked exactly what was done, she said that she could not tell me — I would need to speak to the doctor. However, she said the surgery went well, it was successful, and there were no complications. I also made sure the nurse knew that my mother had ALS and was on a feeding tube, and she said yes, it's all in the chart.

"When can she go home?" I asked.

"I cannot say specifically, but usually, in typical cases, the patients are in the hospital for one to three days, and they get physical therapy."

"I wonder, with her underlying condition, if she might need more care and should be kept there longer."

"That would be up to the doctor," she replied.

I hoped that she would be kept there for a while so that she could get better care. I also wondered if she would need additional home-care assistance once she went home. I didn't think my father realized that when she went home, she would not be just like she was before, she would need even *more* care. I hoped that the hospital would arrange something before she was released.

I let Julie, the caseworker know what was going on. And then I spoke to my brother. Stu said he would also call the nurse and find out more.

A little while later, Stu called me back and said that he had just spoken to the nurse. "Mom is stable and doing well. She is getting pain medication, but she's fine," he said. "She will be getting physical therapy this week. And the hospital will also help arrange home care before she is discharged."

"Good," I replied. "She will need a lot more care than Dad can give her. She will probably need help bathing, getting dressed, and going to the bathroom. She'll need help with everything for a while."

I then spoke to my father and told him the news. "Dad, I highly recommend getting a wheelchair for her. I'd rather she use a wheelchair than keep falling."

"We'll see," he said simply.

"She will need more help than usual when she gets home."

"Yes, I know. Stu told me. We'll be fine."

Julie then called me, concerned about the home health care that my mother would get. She said that the home health assistants would only go to see my mother three days a week, and it might be too much for my father to help her on the other four days. Julie suggested that my mother might be better off in a nursing facility, where she would get care every day, and she said we should discuss this with her doctor.

Ellen also called me to suggest that walking would be good for my mother and that the exercise might help strengthen her legs. She was also concerned that there might be a negative psychological factor if my mother was stuck in a wheelchair all the time. But then she added that if my mother is falling a lot, a wheelchair might be necessary anyway.

A few days later, I left work early and went to visit my mother at the hospital. It was a large, white building, with two wings, and there was a huge parking lot. I was lucky to find a parking spot in the shade of a tree, and I made my way to the main entrance. After getting directions at the information desk, I took the elevator up one floor and found my way to my mother's room. Just as I was approaching her room, I saw my father coming out.

We smiled at each other and hugged. "How is she?" I asked.

"She's fine, she's sleeping now. I've been here since ten o'clock this morning, and I'm going home to eat and take a nap. I'll be back later."

"Perfect, this is like the changing of the guards," I said, smiling, as my father nodded, turned, and walked down the hallway toward the elevator.

I was worried about how my mother would be feeling, so I entered the room timidly. It was a small, private room with a scenic view of a small garden and a distant mountain. She was still sleeping, so I went looking for a nurse to find out the latest about her condition.

"Ruth is doing well," the nurse told me. "All her vital signs are excellent, there are no signs of infection, and everything looks good. She's on morphine, so she's a little out of it right now, but she's doing well."

I thanked her and went back into my mother's room. She opened her eyes as I entered, looked at me, smiled, and then dozed off again. I sat there quietly and let her rest.

Then two physical therapists came and greeted my mother warmly. They helped get her up and out of bed, instructing her on how to move each step of the way. They had her stand up and hold onto a walker. My mother paid attention to and followed all the instructions. It was such a relief to see her standing up and able to put weight on her leg. She walked around the room a little bit and then slowly sat back on the bed and lay back down.

After they left, I held her hand and talked to her awhile. Soon after that, someone came in to take her blood pressure. Then a nurse stopped by to give her a meal through the feeding tube. It seemed that she had constant, warm and caring attention — she was in good hands.

I saw that my mother had a sheet of paper with "yes" and "no" written on it, so the nurses could ask her yes-and-no questions and my mother could point to the answer.

I decided to test it and see how she did. "Mom, how are you feeling? Are you in any pain?"

She held up the paper and pointed behind it, toward the back of the page, so that I could not tell what her answer was.

"Mom, that's not going to help, you need to actually point at something on the front of the paper." She laughed at that.

I then gave her the get-well card that I had brought. Smiling, she read it and then placed it on the little table by her bed. She then closed her eyes and fell back asleep, and I let her rest.

I asked the nurse when they expected to release her. She said, "Hopefully by the end of this week, maybe Friday. And you can discuss with the doctors what type of in-home care she will need, and we will help arrange it."

"Good, thank you. How are her lungs? Does she need a ventilator at all?"

"No, her lungs are fine, there is no problem."

By the time I left, I felt relaxed and had complete trust in the care she was getting.

On Thursday, I found out that they had moved my mother to a rehab facility. She would be able to get more complete physical therapy and rehabilitative care, and she was expected to be there two to three weeks.

That meant that my mother was doing well in her recovery and healing, and she would get round-the-clock care. It also meant that my father would get a break and not have it all on his shoulders. I thought that by the time of her discharge from there, she hopefully would not need as much intensive care anymore, and it would be easier for both of them.

I visited her at the rehab facility, which was housed in one wing of a larger hospital, on Saturday afternoon. She had a private room there as well, even larger than in the previous hospital, with a majestic view of the local mountains. When I entered, I noticed flowers and a large, cheery, get-well balloon. She was awake and smiling. I hugged her, and she hugged back, which felt really good. I rubbed her hands, which brought a smile to her face. I talked to her happily for a little while, and she nodded and responded warmly.

Within a few minutes, the doctor came into the room. He seemed knowledgeable, confident, and kind. I asked him what the diagnosis was and what was done to her hip.

"She had fractured the neck of the femur, just below the head, also called the ball," he explained. "So we replaced the ball, but we did not need to replace the entire socket. So this was a half hip replacement, not a full hip replacement."

I found out that physical therapy (PT) and occupational therapy (OT) workers came in twice a day every day. They got her moving and doing various things to help her recovery. That morning, before I had arrived, they had taken her by wheelchair to the gym on the rehab floor, and she walked a little bit by supporting herself on the parallel bars. She told me that was hard. Then she was returned to her room.

While I was there, PT came back to her room. They moved her legs and feet in various ways so they would not get stiff, and then they had her move them herself, so she would build up her muscle strength.

Shortly after that, I followed them all back to the gym. Once there, my mother carefully got out of the wheelchair and transferred to a walker so that she could take a few steps. She didn't walk far — after a few paces, she was exhausted. They then returned her to her room and put her back in bed, and she immediately dozed off.

During this whole process, I noted that moving her in and out of bed and helping her with the wheelchair was a big ordeal. It took two people to assist her and keep her in a proper position so that her hip would not be strained.

The nurse told me that my mother using the walker was a step up and already an improvement from that morning on the parallel bars. And she was also now able to help more with getting out of bed and moving her body a little on her own, so it wasn't 100 percent on them. I loved hearing that she was already improving and healing.

The PT explained that my mother could not bend more than 90 degrees on that hip or it would dislocate. So they instructed her that when she got in and out of bed, she needed to move like a very pregnant woman with a huge belly. They said that she should lean back and push herself from behind to get up — she could not lean forward. It was awkward, but my mother followed their instructions and did a good job.

My mother was writing more legibly and pointing more easily at words, so communication was clearer this time. She also laughed a few times, which showed me that she was definitely feeling better.

At one point, a nurse came in to check on her, and she asked me what my mother likes to do.

"She likes to read books," I told her.

"Oh," the nurse responded, "what kind of books?"

"Action thrillers and medical thrillers."

My mother handed me a note. "No more medical thrillers for now."

I shared that with the nurse and we all laughed.

The nurse then told me that they expected her to be at this rehab facility at least two weeks, maybe longer. They said that they would evaluate her and decide how long to keep her as she progresses, but they didn't yet know.

It seemed to me that she was being well cared for. I loved that she was up and walking and moving around. And I really liked that my father was visiting her every day, bringing her books and newspapers to read.

But I did notice that her ankles were very stiff. She could not plant her feet flat on the floor; they remained stiffly angled downward and she could not raise them to a 90-degree angle. That meant she could not use the footpads on the wheelchair. I hoped that PT would help her get more flexibility and range of motion back in her ankles. I thought that part of the stiffness might be due to the ALS, but I hoped that the exercises and stretching would at least help a little.

In addition to that problem, we had to think about my mom's home setup. The nurse pulled me aside. "I strongly suggest," she said, "that you get a raised toilet seat for your mother to use at home so that she will not have to sit too low. The low seats are too difficult to get up and down from, and this is especially important recovering from hip surgery."

Stu called me that week to tell me about his visit to see our mother. "I'm very impressed by the hospital she is in," he said. "Every half hour or so, someone else came by to check up on Mom — the nurses, the occupational therapist, the physical therapist, and others. Everyone was very professional and seemed nice. I trust that they will do their best to help Mom."

"That's great," I said. "Very good to hear. And I agree, I found the same thing."

"And her doctor came in while I was there," he continued. "He prescribed an additional anti-depressant for her, which should also help her sleep through the night. And getting enough sleep should also help her mood and overall health."

"Good, I like that," I told him. "Any problems?"

"Well, I was somewhat disturbed by Mom's inability to communicate through writing. She could point to a message board with a 'yes' and a 'no' most of the time, but other times she seemed confused. There were many times when she wanted to communicate, but she wrote in a script that no one could read. I kept asking her to print in big letters. Sometimes she would do that, and then I could read it easily, but then she would revert to illegible script, which was very frustrating. It left me with a strong impression that she's often confused, and unable to understand what she wants. And she had trouble even remembering the need to print."

"I've noticed that, too, and I've also been thinking that she gets confused at times."

"And I tried to get her to use her machine that you type into and says the words. She turned the machine on, but then she refused to press the letters to spell words. This disturbed me, since it seemed that this would help her communicate, and it almost seemed that she didn't really want to communicate or make the effort to help me understand."

"Yeah, I also found she is not using that machine much anymore. Maybe it's getting too difficult or she doesn't remember how to use it."

"I think she is still overwhelmed by the pain in her hip, and the need to adjust the bed height for her comfort. I wrote on a message board 'up,' 'stay,' and 'down' so she could point to how to adjust her bed, and that was helpful. I just hope that as the days go by and her hip heals, that she'll do better at trying to communicate."

"I agree. Her communication has not been good lately, and that makes things so much more difficult. But it hasn't been very good for a while, so I'm not sure how much that will improve. I wish there was more we could do to help."

After hanging up, I tried to relax and trust that she was getting good care and that her hip would heal completely.

23

DEMENTIA AND INFECTION

"Lynn, I just came back from visiting Ruth," Julie told me when she called a few weeks later. "She is doing well, and the nurses and other staff are discussing when to release her. Ruth was good at communicating while I was there, and she wrote down that after she gets released, she will need a wheelchair, an elevated toilet seat, a commode by her bed, and someone to help her. Eric read her notes and just laughed. I did not want to say anything, because I still want to be welcome in their home. But I will make sure the nursing staff discusses all this with both of them when it's time for her to be released."

"Thank you, Julie. I really appreciate all that you are doing."

"Lynn," she added, "I'm worried about Ruth remembering the directions on how to move. I don't want her to move wrong and dislocate that hip and need to have the surgery again. I'm worried that she may forget or not pay attention to all the instructions on how to move."

"We'll make sure," I told her. "I'll go over the instructions again with her. But I think she's good with stuff like that. She should be okay."

Dustin and I went back the next weekend to visit my mother. My stomach felt queasy as we approached her room, not knowing what condition she would be in.

We quietly entered her room in case she was sleeping so we would not disturb her. But she was awake, and she smiled when she saw us. That warmed my heart and melted away some fear. We hugged and she settled back in the bed, at a slight upward angle. She seemed happy, clear, and alert.

"Look, Mom, these are for you." Dustin and I showed her a vase filled with bright pink and yellow flowers, and a big, Mylar get-well balloon. Her smile got bigger. Then I held up a little stuffed bear. It was bright red with little white hearts all over it, and it was fuzzy and squishy. She immediately reached for it, and I handed it to her. She giggled at it, squished it, rubbed its head, and she looked like a happy little kid.

"Mom, how are the nurses? Are they nice to you?"

She nodded yes and wrote a note. "The nurses are very nice, they are kind to me."

"Good, I'm glad. They seem very compassionate and caring."

She looked at the red bear and squished it. Then she wrote a note to me. "But one nurse last night told me to shut up because I was crying."

"What? She told you to shut up?"

"She said to stop crying, that it was disturbing the other patients, but I couldn't stop. So she shut the door so they wouldn't hear me." She held the red squishy bear close to her belly and petted it.

"Oh, Mom. You poor thing. I'm sorry. I'm glad you're feeling better today. And hey — I see you're in your own clothes, not a hospital gown."

"Dad brings me clean clothes every day."

"How nice — that must feel good. Are you walking? Does it hurt to walk?"

"No, it does not hurt to walk, but it is hard."

"Did Julie come to visit you?"

She nodded, smiled, and gave a thumbs-up sign. Then she squeezed her red bear a few more times.

"Are they bathing you?" She gave me a thumbs-up sign.

"Are they bringing you any ice cream?" She laughed and gave a thumbs-down sign, and I laughed with her.

"Mom, look, my skin is so dry, it's cracking. Look at this," I said, and I shoved my thumb in front of her face.

She immediately reached on her table and handed me a tube of petroleum jelly. "Oh Mom, you're still trying to take care of me," I said. She smiled and gave me a thumbs-up sign.

Then I saw her face go blank. "Mom, are you okay? Are you tired?"

There was no response. She pointed to the other side of the room.

"What is it? What do you want?"

She just kept pointing.

"A book?" She shook her head no and pointed again. "The picture?" No. "The flowers?" No. "A blanket?" No.

"Write it down, Mom. I don't know what you want."

She handed me a note. I could not read her handwriting. "Mom, please print, I cannot read this."

She wrote again, more slowly and deliberately, and handed it back. "Ga bom 7, see can."

"Mom, this doesn't make sense."

She wrote more. "Fra mu dot chait."

"Mom, this still doesn't make sense, I can't read this."

She tried again. "Doo stap fish moe la 40,3."

I looked at my mother. She was intently trying to communicate something, but I had no idea what. Something seemed to be scrambled in her brain.

I made more guesses, but they were all wrong. Whatever she wrote down was not intelligible. "Sorry, Mom, I can't understand what you want."

She looked blankly at me and started crying. She ignored the bear.

Then she handed me her note again, with nothing new written on it.

"Mom, I don't know what you're saying."

She looked at her paper, and thrust it at me again, like it might make sense to me if I looked at it one more time.

"Doo stap fish moe la 40,3."

"Sorry, Mom, this doesn't make sense."

She kept crying and handed me the same paper again. I had Dustin look at it, and he couldn't decipher it either.

I pulled my chair closer to her bed and took her hand and held it. And we sat like that for another thirty minutes.

When we left, she was holding the red bear tightly.

One week later, on a warm Saturday, I picked up my father and we went back to the hospital for another visit. This time we found that the door to my mother's room was closed, and a nurse intercepted us. "You need to put on a gown and gloves when you visit her," she said, "and then you need to wash your hands here in this sink after your visit, before you leave."

"Why? What happened?"

"It's for your protection," she said, and she walked away.

We put on the gowns and gloves she handed us. Turning back to the door to open it, we noticed a sheet of paper taped to it with one word written on it: "ISOLATION."

I slowly opened the door and went in. My mother was sitting half-way up in the bed.

"Mom, why do we need to wear a gown and gloves? What happened?"

She wrote a note. "I have MRSA."

"What's that?"

She wrote in clear, large letters, "methicillin-resistant Staphylococcus aureus."

"I don't know what that means."

"Infection. Not good."

"Does it hurt?"

She shook her head no and handed me another note. "Hard to get rid of. Contagious."

"Oh, God." I copied down what she wrote so that I could look it up later on the Internet.

"They are switching my antibiotics to try and get rid of it."

"Let's hope that works."

The door then opened, and a physical therapist came in, wearing a gown and gloves.

"Okay, Sweetie, let's get you up," she said to my mother, placing a wheelchair next to the bed.

My mother swung her legs over the side and got up almost all by herself, with just a little help and some coaching. Then she got into the wheelchair all by herself, while the PT instructed, "Reach behind you, feel for the chair, now sit down."

I followed them out to the hallway and watched as the PT put the walker in front of the chair. My mother slowly got up by herself, reached for the walker, and started walking. I then followed her as she walked all the way down one hallway, over a small bump, and around the outside wall along the windows. She then sat down in the wheelchair to rest, but she only sat for a couple minutes. Then she got up and continued down another long hallway, making a big circle around the floor, and coming all the way back. She went much faster than I expected and looked strong.

Once back in the room, my mother slowly and carefully got back in bed and settled in.

"Wow, Mom, you went fast — I am impressed. You are a speed demon," I told her.

She smiled at me and beamed with pride.

She handed me a note. "PT was here this morning, too. We threw a ball back and forth."

"They really are keeping you active and working your muscles, that is good."

My mother nodded and picked up the red bear with the white hearts all over it. She squished it a few times and held it to her belly.

My father handed my mother a pile of papers. I saw that it was mostly flyers and advertisements that came to their mailbox — stuff that really should be thrown out.

"Mom, Dad is bringing you all the crap to look at."

She laughed and gave me a thumbs-up sign.

"And I bought eight boxes of Cascade for the dishwasher," my father told her.

My mother handed him a note. "Powder or gel?"

"I have no idea," he said. "It said Cascade on the box."

My mother laughed and squeezed her red bear.

"I'm glad you like the bear," I told her.

"That's not a bear, it's a dog," my father said.

"No, it's a bear," I said. Then I saw that my father was joking and just making fun, and my mother was laughing.

The next couple of hours passed quickly. My mother was alert, coherent, and articulate, and she laughed often.

As we got ready to leave, my father kissed my mother good-bye. I wondered if that defeated the purpose of the gowns and gloves, but I decided not to say anything. How could I tell him not to kiss his own wife?

After I got home, I called the hospital and spoke to her nurse. I told her about my father kissing my mother, about the mail that was all over the bed sheets and that my father then picked up that mail and brought it home, and about my father bringing home my mother's dirty clothes to wash. "Is any of that dangerous?" I asked. "Could he catch the infection?"

"No," she answered. "It's okay, as long as he is not touching the wound itself, it's all right. But to be safe, he should put some bleach in the wash when he washes her clothes, and that will kill everything."

I then sent an e-mail to the family back east about the latest with my mother. Ellen called me right away. "That is very disturbing news about MRSA. I wonder if they were not careful enough in the rehab center. It is hard to get rid of the infection, but I have two friends who did. It took a while, but they are both over it. The doctor will just have to try all different drugs to get the right one."

"I don't think I'd blame the hospital," I answered her. "Of course, it's possible, you never know, but they seem so conscientious, and the bug is around anyway. I think Ruthie probably was in a weakened condition so she couldn't fight it off. But you're right, all they need is the right drug and she'll be fine, she'll get over it. Hopefully we'll know later this week if it's responding to the drugs."

Later that week, my father called me. "Your mother is coming home."

"Really? When?"

"This coming Saturday. The doctor will clean out the entire wound area before she comes home so that it is all clean and free from the MRSA."

"Good! Do you know if the MRSA is responding to the new antibiotic?"

"I don't know."

"When you visit tomorrow, ask the nurse."

"Okay, I'll ask tomorrow. They also told me that OT and PT will come home with her to make sure she has everything here that she needs."

I called my father back the next day to check on my mother. "Is she definitely coming home this weekend?"

"Yes, she will be home Saturday morning. And someone from the hospital came yesterday and delivered a wheelchair for her to use. They also installed a high toilet seat to make it easier for her."

"Is the MRSA responding to the antibiotics? Did you ask?"

"I don't know, I didn't ask."

"When she comes home, make sure she moves properly and that the walker is close to her bed."

"Okay," he said.

"I'll come over on Saturday to see her," I told him. "I'll see you then."

On Saturday afternoon, feeling excited and happy, I quickly drove to my parents' house. I got there and rang the bell, but no one answered. I rang again. No answer.

I let myself in with a key and looked around. I peeked in the bathroom, and saw that she had a tall toilet seat that sat over the regular one. It looked sturdy. I went back to the den and sat down, waiting. An hour passed and no one showed up.

I figured that they were simply delayed for some reason and were running late, and I thought that they may have even already left the hospital and would be home any minute. But as it was getting later and I needed to get home, I left a balloon saying "welcome home" in the kitchen, and I wrote a note to let them know that I was there. Then I left and drove home.

Although not overly worried, I was relieved when my father called me later that evening. "Your mother is home," he told me. The doctor showed up late at the hospital. Then she needed a new IV or x-rays or something, I don't know. So we got home at six."

"Is she okay? Did you get her home with no problem?"

"I had trouble getting her in the house. From the car, I got her in a wheelchair and wheeled her to the front door, but I couldn't get the chair over the little step to get into the house."

"So what did you do?"

"I had to finally get her out of the chair and hold the walker to get her in."

"Is she all done with her antibiotics?"

"No, a nurse will come here to the house every day to give her the antibiotics in an IV, so she will complete the medication that way."

"Okay," I said.

"And I told her to wake me up in the night whenever she has to go to the bathroom, so I can help her."

"Good, that's really good, thank you. I'll be there tomorrow to visit."

24

TRYING TO RECOVER

I drove out to their house the next day. I didn't know what to expect, and my stomach was in knots. It felt like it took forever to drive there.

When I finally arrived, I nervously rang the bell, shuffling from foot to foot. My father opened the door.

"Where is she? How is she doing?" I asked right away.

"She's okay. She's in the bedroom," he answered.

I found my mother in bed, a nurse at her side, taking her vital signs. She said that her blood pressure was a bit high, probably because she was in a little pain. After the nurse gave my mother some Advil, she handed my father a prescription to fill for Vicodin and other medications.

The nurse looked at me. "The MRSA has not yet been wiped out. Ruth is no longer on tetracycline, she has now been switched to two other antibiotics, and we hope these will be strong enough to get rid of it."

She then removed the dressing on my mother's hip and looked at the surgical wound. A bit hesitantly, I peeked at my mother's hip. I saw an incision, maybe six inches long, with staples holding it closed. It looked nice and clean to me. It was a little pink in one area where the infection was. The nurse wiped the entire area with Betadine and put on a new clean dressing.

The nurse then handed me her card and explained that she was not sent by the hospital, but that she was from a home-care nursing group. As the case manager for my mother, she would oversee all the at-home nursing care. A nurse would come out every day to check on my mother, hook up an IV to her arm, and give her the meds she needed. She also explained that other nurses might come, but she would be the one visiting the house most of the time, and she would manage and oversee everything, including the other nurses.

As the nurse also explained that OT and PT would come out this week and evaluate her and determine how often to come out and what to do, my mother started crying softly.

"Mom, this is temporary, and each day will get easier."

She continued crying softly, her head buried in the covers on the bed.

Then the nurse turned, the rust-colored medication in her raised hand, and as she moved she accidentally spilled some of the liquid. I went over to look and saw that it had dripped onto the white comforter and the carpeting. The nurse apologized a few times, and I ran and got wet paper towels and wiped up what I could, but it did not all come out. I hoped the rest of the stain would come out later when it got washed.

As soon as the nurse left, my father went to the pharmacy and filled the four prescriptions. I stayed and sat with my mother. When she asked for it, I helped her roll onto her side and propped her there with a pillow behind her back. I then brought her the little squishy red bear, which she laid down on its side, facing her, right next to her face. Within a minute, she had fallen asleep in that position. While she slept, I brought the welcome-home balloon into her bedroom and put it at the foot of her bed, so when she would look up, she would see it.

As my mother continued to doze, I closed my eyes and rested, grateful for a few moments of peace.

My father returned shortly after that, and we looked at the medications that he was given. I then looked at the paper listing the prescriptions and noticed that none of them matched. I looked at the pill bottles, thinking maybe they would indicate that they were generic, but I didn't see anything. So I told my father to call the pharmacy and ask them which was which, so he could match them to his list. I also told him that the next time he goes to the pharmacy, to ask for easy-open caps.

I then relayed to him a message from the nurse, telling him that when my mother wakes up, to give her a pain pill, and then another one before bed at night, and he said okay.

After a few more minutes, and seeing that my mother was resting comfortably, I went home, with my stomach feeling a bit unsettled.

I called my father from work the next day. He told me that he had gone back to the pharmacy after I had left, and the pharmacist showed him which pill was which on his list, so he was able to match them all up. He also said he gave my mother the pain pills as instructed, and that she was doing better.

"Here, I'll let you talk to her," he said and I heard muffled noises coming over the phone.

"Hi, Mom," I said. I could hear her labored breathing. "I hope you are feeling better today. I love you."

After listening to her breathing for another minute, I heard my father come back on the phone, and he told me that she had fallen back asleep.

That week, I printed signs with big words on them — yes, no, pain, bathroom, etc. — so my mother could point to the words and communicate, like she did in the hospital. I taped them on cardboard so they would be sturdy and easier to use.

A couple days later, I called and spoke to my father. "How is Mom doing?"

"A nurse is coming here every day to put meds in the IV. And OT and PT have been coming and getting your mother up walking and doing various exercises. So that's good."

"Is she still in pain?"

"She's doing fine. In fact, I took her to a jazz concert last night."

"What? She's not ready for something like that."

"She's fine, it was wonderful, and your mother loved it."

"She's barely walking — you can't do that to her. That's too soon."

"It was wonderful and we had a good time."

I hung up in frustration, hoping that it truly hadn't been too much for her. I wished she would just tell him "no" when he wanted to take her to places like that if she wasn't up for it.

I sent an e-mail to family in New York, updating them with the latest news. I heard back from Ellen and Fran, both of whom said that they were planning to come to California to visit in April. I looked forward to seeing them, but even more important, I knew that seeing her sisters would be great for my mother's morale and recovery.

The next Saturday, I went back to visit with my mother. When I first got there, she was lying in bed. As soon as I said hi to her, she started crying and wailing. To help her communicate, I gave her the printed sheets and a pretty pink clipboard to hold them. She put them on the bed next to her and continued to sob.

About a half hour later, a nurse showed up to give my mother her antibiotics. My mother sat up and got out of bed cautiously. Leaning on her walker, she slowly shuffled into the den. Then she sat down in her wheelchair, and the nurse hooked up an IV.

The nurse explained that my mother was now getting a different antibiotic, and she was scheduled to get this antibiotic daily, through the IV, for a month.

"Is the MRSA responding to it?" I asked her.

"We won't know until she's tested again, which will be this coming week," the nurse answered. "It's actually very common for patients to get this in the hospitals and some patients never get rid of it. For some people, their body just adjusts to it, and they become carriers of it, but they never get rid of it."

"What else are you giving her?"

"That's all I'm giving her by IV, just the antibiotics," she said, and she smiled at my mother and patted her arm.

The nurse then checked my mother's pulse and blood pressure, and she told me that her blood pressure was now back down and was within a normal range.

"Okay, I'll be back tomorrow," she said, as she packed up her things and left.

Once the nurse was gone, my mother seemed calm and relaxed.

"Do you feel up to a short walk?" I asked her.

She nodded. Standing up tentatively, she held onto her walker. My mom, my dad, and I made our way to the front door and slowly left the house. My mother held tightly to the walker and shuffled down the driveway to the sidewalk. It was a warm, sunny day, and my mother squinted into the bright light. We walked slowly down the sidewalk, my mother leaning into the walker, a soft breeze rustling the fine hair on her head. It was good to see her smiling again. We made it to the next house, and then my mother sat and rested on the seat attached to the walker.

"This is healthy for you," I told her. "It's nice to get out in the fresh air and sunshine and walk a little. This will strengthen your muscles and help your joint heal. And it's especially important that you enjoy your days and do things that make you smile."

My mother nodded.

"I'll take her out for a walk every day," my father offered.

Then my mother stood up, grabbed onto the walker, and we turned and walked back to their house.

Once we were back, I looked at my mother. "I see you keep a pillow between your legs when you sit on the wheelchair."

She handed me a note. "It helps my hip align better and is more comfortable." Then she added, "I'm okay. Don't worry about me."

"I will not be able to come out next weekend," I told her. "Since I'm working at an accounting office, and it's tax season, we're really busy right now, and I need to work next Saturday." My mother nodded. "I've been working a lot of overtime plus

Saturdays, and I'm really exhausted. So I won't be here next weekend, but I'll be here in two weeks. Okay?" She nodded again.

"And in two weeks, your two sisters are coming out from New York to visit, so we'll all be here together then. It will be nice."

The following day, I received a call from a social worker. "I was out to visit Ruth," she said. "I'm concerned that she will need ongoing care. Once these nursing visits end, she will still need someone to go out there and help her."

She then gave me the names and telephone numbers of three agencies we could call if needed.

Then the PT called me. "I'm worried about Ruth," she said right away. "Eric was gone all afternoon, and he can't leave her alone like that for that long. It's not safe and Ruth was upset," she said. I could hear my mother crying in the background.

"Okay, I'll talk to my father," I promised.

I then called my father. "I was told that you left Mom alone all afternoon," I told him.

"I needed a break," he said. "It's only once a week, every Monday, and I'm only gone three hours. I play bridge every Monday afternoon, and the nurse and PT were here, so she wasn't alone for long."

"Maybe she shouldn't be alone much at all yet," I said.

"She is more independent now and can get around okay. She can also go to the bathroom by herself and walk around. She's fine, it's not a big deal." He paused and then added, "And I need a break. It's only once a week. I'm not canceling my bridge game."

"Okay," I responded, "I understand what you're saying. I know you do a lot for her, and yes, you deserve to do something fun for yourself once a week."

"And she doesn't need constant care," he added. "She's fine."

I hoped he was right.

25

Neglect and Abandonment

After I hung up, I thought about what my father had said. I knew that the PT and social worker were responding to my mother crying, but I also knew that she cried a lot anyway, as part of her disease. And I also knew that my father really was doing a lot for her, and my mother exaggerated when she said that my father did not pay attention to her and neglected her. So telling him that he could never leave the house was not realistic or appropriate.

I immediately called Julie, the caseworker, to discuss it with her.

"What concerns me, Lynn," Julie said right away, "is that Eric is leaving during the day throughout the week to go to the gym, or join friends, or to play cards for a couple of hours each time, leaving Ruth at home alone multiple times. If he is unwilling to hire a companion caregiver for the times he is gone, he needs to ask a neighbor or friend to stay with Ruth while he is out. If Eric does not do this, Lynn, he needs to be reported to the Adult Protective Services Division of the County Human Services Department. Ruth is considered an elder disabled dependent adult and needs full-time supervision due to her decreasing physical and mental abilities. Especially now that she is less able, since she fractured her hip."

I felt a sinking feeling in my stomach, and my voice was soft. "What if my father left for just an hour? If he runs to the grocery store, does he really need to call in an aide first? That seems excessive to me. If my mother can walk around by herself and go to the bathroom by herself, does she really need constant 24-hour care?"

"Lynn, Eric leaves throughout the day whenever he wants. I'm concerned that Ruth is left alone too much. And what if there is a problem?"

"Well, she certainly should not be left alone for hours at a time, but one hour here or there should not be that big of a deal. Maybe she should have an aide scheduled just for the once a week that he plays bridge for three hours, or whenever he has a block of time away greater than one hour. Would that be acceptable?"

"We can see if that would work."

"I would hate to report him, as he is really doing a lot, on a constant daily basis, to help her. To tell him that to leave for an hour constitutes legal or medical neglect seems awfully harsh and a slap in the face to him. I will discuss this with both of them and see what they agree to, and I'll get back to you. And thank you for expressing your concerns about this and giving me more information about it."

I then talked to my brother and my mother's two sisters. After discussing it in depth, we all agreed that if my father was gone for an hour or less, that would be okay. But for more than an hour, he should arrange someone to come in and sit with her.

"But we need to include Dad in the decision-making process so that he's part of this," I told Stu. "We can't just dictate it to him.

We need to make it seem like we're helping *him* as well as helping *her*, and that he agrees with it."

"Yes," he answered, "but don't forget that Dad is still in denial of her condition, and he is overestimating her abilities. And he is underestimating the amount of care she needs. She's not just recovering from surgery; she has a severe underlying condition. I think she needs more help than he is admitting or recognizing."

"You're right. She's really not that independent. She still needs help getting up and down from a chair. And she still gets confused. Sometimes she's clear and sometimes she's not. Dad is not being realistic."

"And I'm concerned that in the meantime," he continued, "before this gets worked out, Dad will be going to play tennis for over an hour, to the gym for over an hour, and to play bridge for three hours. He's actually gone a lot more than he's saying, and we need to take care of this as soon as possible."

"Yeah, you're right. When I had mentioned to Dad that he can't leave Mom alone, he said, 'Yes I can, she's okay, and I need a break.' He was defiant about it. So we need to make sure he understands that we're not trying to take away his free time or fun activities, we just need to arrange other coverage while he's away. And we need to take care of this soon. Monday is his next bridge game, and that's for three hours."

Fran then called me. "I spoke to Eric last night and he said when he plays tennis or works out, he does that in the mornings after he takes care of Ruthie. He said that she goes back to bed before he leaves, so he feels she is safe there. The only problem is really when he plays bridge."

I then heard from Julie, the caseworker. "The problem with this whole issue is that Eric is not abusing or neglecting Ruth, but it does border on neglect and abandonment when he leaves her alone. According to the description in a booklet written by the Elder Abuse Council, abandonment is when a dependent adult or elderly person, unable to care for him or herself, is left alone by the person having the responsibility to take care of that person. Neglect also includes a caregiver's failure to protect the elderly person from health and safety hazards."

"I understand what you're saying, and we're trying to find someone to be there with her when Eric plays bridge."

"Lynn, as you know, I have encouraged Eric and Ruth many times to hire some additional in-home caregiving services this past year. I believe it would have made their lives so much easier. In some ways, I think Eric takes pride in the fact that he is doing it all. Even Ruth wrote down for me while I visited her in the hospital that she would need more help at home."

"I know, but when we tried a few times to get people in to help, both my parents said no, and we did not want to force it on them if they didn't want it."

"My bigger concern is that I feel at this time Ruth has dementia or diminished mental capacity. She is sometimes lucid and sometimes not, and in an emergency with no one there, she would not know what to do. Eric is taking a big risk every time he leaves her alone for several hours. Personally, I think Ruth would actually enjoy having a female caregiver with her once in a while. It might feel like a friend to her."

"Okay, I will talk to them again."

"In the meantime, I have suggested that Eric meet with the senior care consultant from the local healthcare district. She may be able to help find a part-time caregiver for Ruth or have other resources where she could direct your family. Please keep me informed."

After I hung up, I felt a heavy despair welling up in me, and I convulsed into sobs.

26

THE PHONE CALL

On a Tuesday in early April 2009, I came home from work exhausted, after doing a few intense hours of overtime. I felt overcome with fatigue. I collapsed in a chair, trying to decide what to eat for dinner, too tired to move.

The phone rang, and it was my brother. "Hi, Stu," I said when I heard his voice.

"Hi," he said quietly. "Did you speak to Dad? Did you hear?"

"No, I just got home. What is it?"

There was a pause. "Mom passed away last night." Another pause. "Dad said she was fine when she went to bed, but she never woke up."

"Oh my God." I held tightly to the phone.

"He doesn't know what to do." Stu took a few breaths. "I told him who to call. We'll have to arrange a memorial service and a funeral."

"Oh my God," I said again. I took a deep breath and rubbed my forehead, unable to say anything else.

My brother continued. "We'll have the memorial service here in California this weekend, and then we'll ship her body back to New York and have the funeral there next week. I'll come down there on Friday and help arrange everything."

I called my father. His voice sounded quiet and strained when he answered. "Dad, I just heard. I'm so sorry."

"Yeah, she died last night." His voice was barely audible.

"I need to eat something, I just got home. Then I'll come out there."

"You don't have to come now, it's late. I'm okay. Come tomorrow."

"When did she die?"

"I don't know. It must have been soon after she went to bed last night. She never got up during the night to go to the bathroom like she usually does. And then when I got up this morning and looked at her, I knew."

"I'm glad she went peacefully in the middle of the night."

"Me, too."

The next morning, I went to my dad's house and stayed with him all day. In between the silence, we discussed how much she had suffered.

"I think it was all just too much for her and she was ready to go," I told him.

He kept looking at pictures of her, his eyes filled with tears. I walked into their bedroom and saw that the red squishy bear was still on her side of the bed, and a powerful sob filled me.

As I turned to leave the bedroom, I saw my mother's purse sitting open on her dresser. I walked over to close it, and as I glanced inside, I saw a folded piece of paper. Curious, I took it out and unfolded it. Printed on it, in my mother's handwriting, were three words: "I have ALS." I gasped and realized that this was her message to any medical personnel who might find her body or need to treat her. I put the paper down, sat down shakily, covered my face with my hands, and dissolved into tears.

After I got home, I started thinking about what I wanted to say at the upcoming memorial service and funeral. There was a lot to do to prepare for these gatherings, and I wasn't sure where to start.

But first things first. I looked through all my pictures, collecting my favorite photos of my mom when she was healthy, and I quickly put together a small photo album. Two days later, I went back to visit my dad, and I gave him the photo album with pictures of his wife. He held the album tenderly, his eyes wet with tears, carefully flipping the pages, absorbed in each picture. He looked at me and said, "I still walk around the house saying, 'Ruthie, where are you?'" He closed his eyes for a few moments and then slowly opened them. Then he started looking through the pictures again.

Friends and family filled the chapel to overflowing for the memorial service, and I was impressed at the number of people from my parents' retirement community who attended, especially since it was difficult for many of them to get around.

My father was dazed and disoriented, and I sat in the front row next to him and held his hand throughout most of the service, until it was my turn to speak.

My mother had written a letter to her family and friends shortly before she passed away. I read this letter aloud to everyone in attendance. My voice cracked as I recited her words, and I could only get out a few words at a time, but I managed to read it all. It was heartfelt, open, and loving. She spoke of forgiveness and love. She spoke of life and illness and asked everyone to remember her the way she was when she was healthy. She spoke to family and friends, telling everyone how much she loved them.

After I finished and looked up, I saw people dabbing at their eyes. As I sat back down in my seat, I was overcome with a mixture of anguish, connection, grief, and love, and I realized that my mother was still reaching out and touching others, even after her death.

The cloudy sky threatened rain in New York the following week as we made our way to the cemetery. Our family gathered there — my father, Stu, Ellen and Adam, Fran, Dustin and me, and my cousins. We greeted each other in hushed tones, and then huddled around the open grave. Many of us had written short speeches, and we took turns reading them to each other in our intimate group. We shared heartfelt and loving memories, some of which made us laugh, and some of which made us cry.

I read my speech slowly, haltingly. My voice cracked. My hands visibly shook the page and made the words jump before my eyes.

We watched the casket as it was lowered into the ground, and we dropped in rose petals, as prayers were chanted. I could not stop the tears, nor did I want to. Finally, feeling empty and drained, all I could do was clutch at my prayer booklet and look up at the billowing gray clouds above us. After the conclusion of the graveside service, we made our way to Fran's house for food and togetherness, finding solace in each other's company.

It hit me how much we take for granted, and how deep the loss is once someone is gone. I wished I could take away the illness, make her healthy, and have my mom back.

Oh, Mom, you were truly a gift to this world. I love and miss you more than you could ever know.

Epilogue

It is now 2014, and five years have passed since we buried my mom. My father often tells me that my mother visits him in his dreams and that they have long, detailed conversations, which he loves.

I heard from many of my mother's friends, telling me how she had helped them over the years, and how easy she was to be with and talk to. I got to see another side of her that I never knew before, and it made me miss her even more.

I have gone to New York a few times to visit Fran, Ellen and Adam, and my cousins. But each time I go back there, I feel overcome with new waves of grief. Too much is missing when she's not there. How could I visit my mom's family without my mom? I hoped she was somehow still there with us, seeing us all together.

My father gradually became more calm and relaxed, happy, and easy-going. He now laughs freely, and he often gets silly and goofy. He is always happy to see me and is very loving and caring.

My brother and I have also noticed that my father has recently been getting forgetful and confused. He does not remember to show up for doctor appointments. Once he went back a second time, unaware that he was just there the day before. His bills often go unpaid, yet he insists that they're all taken care of. He often mixes up his sentences and forgets common vocabulary.

We took him to his doctor for an evaluation. After the visit, we were informed that my father has Alzheimer's.

In February 2014, my father celebrated his 90th birthday. He stopped driving, and Stu and I have begun the process of moving him into a dementia-care facility near me where he will be well cared for, and where I can visit him often.

I think of my mother every day, and I imagine her the way she was before she got sick. I often look at my photos of her, treasuring each picture, missing her deeply, and sending her my love.

Many times I visualize her smiling and happy, surrounded by hearts, rainbows, rose petals, and loving pink light. I often sit quietly and visit her in my mind and heart, and I imagine giving her a big bear hug, and I swear I can feel her hug me back.

ADDENDUM

After years of involvement, I have learned a lot about ALS and about what might be helpful and supportive to patients with this disease. I would like to share a bit of what I have discovered. In the spirit of simply reaching out to help others, I offer the following practical suggestions for ALS patients and their families, friends, and caregivers.

Please understand that I am not a licensed physician, nor do I practice medicine. I am by no means offering medical advice, and the following is not meant as a substitution or replacement for regular medical treatment. If you are under a physician's care, please continue to follow the advice of your doctor. Please use the following tips based on your own judgment and at your own risk.

1. You are not alone. No matter what you are experiencing or feeling, there are countless other patients facing similar situations and difficulties. Many other ALS patients and families share your pain and troubles, so remember that you are not alone with your battle.

2. Always remember that you are not your body, you are not your disease, and you are not your symptoms. You are still the loving, caring, smart, fun, sweet, amazing, and special person inside that you always were and always will be. Despite any disease or illness, you are still worthwhile and valuable. You are loved.

3. Find and surround yourself with a network of support. Don't isolate yourself. If possible, locate an ALS support group in your area and attend meetings. Or search for organizations or support groups online. They can help answer questions, give suggestions, share referrals, and offer emotional understanding and compassion. This type of assistance is invaluable.

4. Ask for assistance. Let people in, let people help you physically, emotionally, and with various tasks. You should not try to face and deal with everything alone. Don't let pride stand in your way, and don't try to tough it out all by yourself. People who know you and care about you *want* to help — let them. Most people won't know what you need help with — so tell them. Ask for what you need.

5. Please make your wishes known — as long as you are able to clearly state your wishes, you *always* have final say about what care you receive and which assistive devices you use. Nothing should be forced on you. It is completely up to you when or if you choose to use assistive devices such as feeding tubes, BiPAP machines, or respirators. Some patients want these devices and some don't — it's different for everyone, and it is based on your own experience, discomfort, and lifestyle choices. And to all family, friends, and caregivers: Please respect the patient's decisions and requests. These are personal choices and should be honored.

6. Remember, you have a say about what measures are taken to extend your life. It's up to you whether you want a do-not-resuscitate (DNR) order in place. A DNR is a request not to be resuscitated if your heart stops or if you stop breathing. Without a DNR, hospital staff will try to help a patient whose heart or breathing has stopped. Also, fill out advance health-care directives and make your end-of-life wishes known while you can.

It is important to have those things in writing so that your choices and preferences for care can be followed when you can't speak for yourself. You can get health-care directive forms at your doctor's office, local hospital, or through places such as *www.fivewishes.org*.

7. Find joy and happiness wherever you can and in whatever makes you smile. Yes, there will be time for anger and frustration and the grieving process, but don't let that dominate every moment or be all that there is. Seek pleasure in things you still can do that make you feel good — whether that's walking, reading, sitting in nature among the trees and flowers, or watching birds or sunsets. Savor and cherish your relationships with friends and family. Find wonder in the little things — those can end up being the big things, and they can bring more depth and meaning to your life.

8. Always treat yourself with tenderness, love, and compassion. You have a lot to deal with, and you deserve all the love that's possible, especially from yourself. To family, friends, and caregivers: Always treat the patient with as much kindness, compassion, patience, and love as feasible. This often makes a huge and powerful difference in the patient's life.

9. To all caregivers: Please be kind and gentle with yourself as well. Have relief caregivers back you up so that you can get away and have time off. Take care of yourself — make sure you get enough rest and that you take time to do things that bring you joy. If needed, find a support group for caregivers, where you can share your feelings and feel understood and supported.

10. To all patients, all caregivers, and to each person reading this now: Please love yourself completely — your body, your strength, your wisdom, your kind heart, your humor, and

everything that is *you*. Treasure being alive each moment. And always love who you are — because deep inside, you *are* love.

For more information on ALS, to find a chapter in your area, or to make a donation, please visit *www.alsa.org*.

I genuinely wish each of you much love and peace, from all of my heart to all of yours.

PICTURES

The author shares with you a few pictures of the family.

Ruthie 1985:

Ruthie 1998:

Ruthie 2002:

"Eric" and Ruthie 1946:

Ruthie and "Eric" 1997:

Ruthie and "Eric" 1997:

"Eric" and Ruthie 2002:

The three sisters
"Ellen", Ruthie, and "Fran" – 2002:

Lynn (the author)
and Ruthie 2007:

Back row – "Fran", "Eric", "Adam", and "Ellen"
Front row seated – Ruthie 2007:

"Stu" and "Brenda" 2011:

"Adam" and "Ellen" 2013:

"Fran" 2015:

"Dustin" and Lynn (the author and her husband) 2015:

Sweet, beautiful Ruthie in 2002
Ruthie wanted to be remembered how she was
when she was healthy.
This is how the author remembers her:

ABOUT THE AUTHOR

LYNN MICLEA is a writer, author, editor, musician, Reiki master practitioner, and dog lover.

After retiring, Lynn further pursued her passion for writing, and she is now a successful author with many books published and more on the way.

She has written numerous short stories and published many books including thrillers, science fiction, paranormal, romance, mystery, memoirs, a grammar guide, self-help guided imagery, short story collections, and children's stories (fun animal stories about kindness, believing in yourself, and helping others).

She hopes that through her writing she can help empower others, stimulate people's imagination, and open new worlds as she entertains with powerful and heartfelt stories and helps educate people with her nonfiction books.

Originally from New York, Lynn currently lives in Southern California with her loving and supportive husband.

Please visit *www.lynnmiclea.com* for more information.

BOOKS BY LYNN MICLEA

Fiction

New Contact

Transmutation

Journey Into Love

Ghostly Love

Guard Duty

Loving Guidance

The Diamond Murders

The Finger Murders

The Sticky-Note Murders

Short Story Collections

Beyond the Abyss – Science Fiction

Beyond Terror – Thrillers, Horror, and Suspense

Beyond Love – Love and Romance

Beyond Connections – Family and Intimacy

Non-Fiction

Grammar Tips & Tools

Ruthie: A Family's Struggle with ALS

Mending a Heart: A Journey Through Open-Heart Surgery

Unleash Your Inner Joy – Volume 1: Peace

Unleash Your Inner Joy – Volume 2: Abundance

Unleash Your Inner Joy – Volume 3: Healing

Unleash Your Inner Joy – Volume 4: Spirituality

Children's Books

Penny Gains Confidence

Sammy and the Fire

Sammy Visits a Hospital

Sammy Meets Grandma

Sammy Goes to the Dog Park

Sammy Falls in Love

Sammy and the Earthquake

Sammy Goes On Vacation

Wish Fish: Book 1 – Discovering the Secret

Wish Fish: Book 2 – Endless Possibilities

One Last Thing...

Thank you for reading this book — I hope you loved it!

If you enjoyed this book, I'd be very grateful if you would post a short review on Amazon. Your support really makes a big difference and helps me immensely!

Simply click the "leave-a-review" link for this book at Amazon, and leave a short review. It would mean a lot to me!

Thank you so much for your support—it is very appreciated!

Thank You!